The Macat Library
世界思想宝库钥匙丛书

解析保罗·肯尼迪

《大国的兴衰：1500—2000年的经济变革与军事冲突》

AN ANALYSIS OF

PAUL KENNEDY'S

THE RISE AND FALL OF THE GREAT POWERS

Economic Change and Military
Conflict from 1500-2000

Riley Quinn ◎ 著

王晋瑞◎译

上海外语教育出版社
外教社 SHANGHAI FOREIGN LANGUAGE EDUCATION PRESS

MACAT

目　录

引 言　……………………………………………………………　1

　　保罗·肯尼迪其人　　　　　　　　　　　　　　2

　　《大国的兴衰》的主要内容　　　　　　　　　3

　　《大国的兴衰》的学术价值　　　　　　　　　4

第一部分：学术渊源　………………………………………　7

　　1. 作者生平与历史背景　　　　　　　　　　　8

　　2. 学术背景　　　　　　　　　　　　　　　　13

　　3. 主导命题　　　　　　　　　　　　　　　　18

　　4. 作者贡献　　　　　　　　　　　　　　　　22

第二部分：学术思想　………………………………………　27

　　5. 思想主脉　　　　　　　　　　　　　　　　28

　　6. 思想支脉　　　　　　　　　　　　　　　　33

　　7. 历史成就　　　　　　　　　　　　　　　　38

　　8. 著作地位　　　　　　　　　　　　　　　　43

第三部分：学术影响　………………………………………　47

　　9. 最初反响　　　　　　　　　　　　　　　　48

　　10. 后续争议　　　　　　　　　　　　　　　53

　　11. 当代印迹　　　　　　　　　　　　　　　57

　　12. 未来展望　　　　　　　　　　　　　　　62

术语表　……………………………………………………………　66

人名表　……………………………………………………………　73

CONTENTS

WAYS IN TO THE TEXT 81

    Who Is Paul Kennedy?   82

    What Does *The Rise and Fall of the Great Powers* Say?   83

    Why Does *The Rise and Fall of the Great Powers* Matter?   85

SECTION 1: INFLUENCES 87

    Module 1: The Author and the Historical Context   88

    Module 2: Academic Context   94

    Module 3: The Problem   100

    Module 4: The Author's Contribution   105

SECTION 2: IDEAS 111

    Module 5: Main Ideas   112

    Module 6: Secondary Ideas   118

    Module 7: Achievement   124

    Module 8: Place in the Author's Work   129

SECTION 3: IMPACT 135

    Module 9: The First Responses   136

    Module 10: The Evolving Debate   142

    Module 11: Impact and Influence Today   147

    Module 12: Where Next?   153

Glossary of Terms 158

People Mentioned in the Text 166

Works Cited 171

引言

要 点

- 英国历史学家保罗·肯尼迪出生于 1945 年，其职业生涯主要在美国度过，冷战 * 后期开始在学术上享有盛名（冷战是美国和苏联 * 关系紧张的特殊历史时期，始于二战结束，止于 1991 年欧洲共产主义 * 瓦解）。

- 作者在《大国的兴衰》（1987）一书中指出，奠定大国统治地位的主要条件是经济实力，而非军事实力。

- 作者在书中还提出了美国在未来很可能会走向衰落这一重要观点；书中的总结性观点引发了人们的争论，并且至今仍在继续。

保罗·肯尼迪其人

　　《大国的兴衰》（1987）的作者保罗·肯尼迪是一位英国历史学家，1945 年出生于英格兰北部一个普通的工薪家庭。他是家中第一个上大学的人，毕业于纽卡斯尔大学 * 历史学专业，获一等荣誉学位。在牛津大学 * 获得博士学位后，保罗·肯尼迪移居美国，任耶鲁大学 * 国际关系史研究室主任。

　　在全球政治格局极不稳定的时期，《大国的兴衰》这样一部有关大国政治著作的出版非常及时。该书于 1987 年出版，没过几年，冷战即宣告结束，国际格局也随之发生了转变。冷战期间，全球局势高度紧张，美国和苏联一直处于暗中角力的状态，两国都想通过发展核武器和插手第三方的战争来制约对方，但彼此存在的敌意并未引发公开冲突。20 世纪 80 年代末，美国发起了新一轮挑衅性攻势，苏联也相应增加了预算，以应对来自美国的威胁。

　　保罗·肯尼迪凭借《大国的兴衰》一书在学术界和文学界赢得

了一定的知名度，他还因此成了一位著述颇丰的国际事务评论家。他的学术研究主要关注的是国际机构（如联合国＊）的重要性。他撰写的有关大国政治方面的文章，一些发表在通俗出版物上，一些则发表在诸如《外交事务》＊等外交政策方面的专业性期刊上。

《大国的兴衰》的主要内容

保罗·肯尼迪在《大国的兴衰》一书中指出，全球大国的兴衰变化有固定的规律可循。他从 1500 年的欧洲谈起，从两个方面分析了当时统治整个欧洲的哈布斯堡王朝＊。当时，这个有着奥地利和西班牙血脉的声名显赫的家族成员在欧洲位高权重。肯尼迪认为哈布斯堡王朝日渐衰落的原因是其在军事上的投入已远远超出了其经济实力。换言之，哈布斯堡王朝在我们今日看来已是"强弩之末"时发动了太多的战争，最终令其财政不堪重负。经济实力的下降削弱了其军事实力，而军事实力下降又造成了经济的进一步衰退。

因此，肯尼迪认为大国的军事战略和经济实力是决定其兴衰成败的重要因素。他用同样的范式＊（概念模型）分析了随后几个世纪里西、法、英、德、美等大国的情况。但肯尼迪并不是一个"唯经济决定论者"，他认为历史大事并不是由经济状况预先决定的。不过，他认为一个国家占有的经济资源越多，该国政治家的政策选择也就越多。随着时间的推移，有更多政策选择权的国家则会变得更加繁荣，也就更有可能超越其他的国家。

《大国的兴衰》之所以被视为一部重要著作，并非因为该书对 16 世纪的世界格局分析得十分到位，而是因为该书最后的预测性章节用历史经验告诉我们 20 世纪大国的走向。肯尼迪预言，美国有可能会遭遇那些老牌帝国曾经的命运：由于军事投入超出其经济承受能力，美国会面临衰落的危险。但纵观 20 世纪 90 年代，美国在世界上的领导地位不可撼动，该预言也就没有那么深入人心。

21 世纪初，美国在全球的领导地位开始动摇。2001 年 9 月 11 日的恐怖袭击事件（9·11 事件）*让美国延长了其在发展中国家驻军的计划；而与此同时，中国为世界经济发展所做出的贡献也越来越大。2007—2008 年的全球金融危机过后，肯尼迪的观点再次得到了学者们的关注：美国在走向衰落吗？美国在对外政策上也开始进入了内省阶段：是该增加海外投入以应对新兴大国的挑战呢，还是该减少海外投入以保证目前占有的资源不再继续减少呢？

争论还远未结束，而争论愈是激烈，世界将愈加动荡不定。

《大国的兴衰》的学术价值

《大国的兴衰》对过去五百年间世界上发生的重大历史事件进行了详细梳理。但肯尼迪认为，历史不仅仅是对一系列事件的简单罗列，他还需要去**解释**这些事件发生的原因。我们能从历史事件中发现什么规律？引发事件的内在原因又是什么？《大国的兴衰》能帮助读者更好地理解历史事件发生的**前因后果**，是一本了解史学和政治学研究的重要参考书。

该书还能让读者学会用敏锐的视角去解读当下的时事问题。决策者和专家们一直在争论一个问题：现在的美国到底是否处于衰退期？《大国的兴衰》给出的回答是——可能如此。但作者也指出，"衰落主义"*认为任何国家都会不可避免地经历衰退期，但用这一思想来说明美国的状况就是把问题简单化了。一国的衰退难道就只是个经济学问题吗？和"国家身份"就没有关系吗？全球领导者的地位值得煞费苦心地去争取吗？

我们需要用批判性思维去看待"衰落主义"的两种解释方法，即大规模的历史分析法和共时观察法。此外，《大国的兴衰》让读者明白了为什么一种方法比另一种方法更容易让人接受。"衰落主义"的解释基础是否成立？典型的"帝国过度投入"就是一国出于自身安全考虑，承担起了管理外国领土的任务。冷战期间和冷战之后的美国对外政策一直是包括肯尼迪在内的一些思想家所关注的问题，他们认为美国的外交策略是不够谨慎的。

今天，有不少人认为，美国应该对叙利亚、俄罗斯等国家的某些行为进行一定程度的干预。《大国的兴衰》为读者描绘出了不同决策从长远来看会带来的不同结果：干预会有过度投入的风险，不干预会有失去发言权的风险。该书为我们提供了验证某些断言的方法，对那些天马行空、缺乏论证的假说尤为适用。

第一部分：学术渊源

1 作者生平与历史背景

要点 🔑

- 《大国的兴衰》认为，一个国家的军事优势一定是建立在其经济比其他国家都要繁荣这一基础上的。

- 肯尼迪的历史研究对统治世界的伟大帝国（近年来，对国际组织）产生了浓厚的兴趣。

- 《大国的兴衰》出版于全球局势紧张的冷战后期，也正是在该时期，美国在"里根主义"*（即增加军费开支以遏制苏联）的思想指导下，加强了其在海外的军事投入。

为何要读这部著作？

保罗·肯尼迪的《大国的兴衰》从宏观的视角来分析历史。该书的时间跨度始于现代民族国家开始诞生的 1500 年的欧洲王朝权力争夺（各贵族间的争权夺利），终于冷战行将结束之际。《大国的兴衰》出版于 1987 年；四年后，苏联解体，冷战也随之结束。作者并不是简单地在按时间顺序罗列历史上发生的事件，而是试图去解释互为对手的国家是如何凭借自身的经济实力来影响战争走向、制定外交策略的。

一个国家如果能够在经济上蓬勃发展，在技术上不断进步，在军事上不过度投入，那么在**与其他国家的竞争中**就能脱颖而出。相反，"帝国过度投入"行为则可能会使原本的强国失去其领导地位：随着战略投入加大，自信心得到提升，军队规模也会随之扩大；但经济发展如果无法跟上战略投入的步伐，"大国"也终将走向衰落。

8

作者用相同的方法分析了 15 世纪至 19 世纪的西班牙帝国、大英帝国＊以及现代美国的发展趋势。

> "（美国要想）遏制并终结苏联的扩张，就需要与其在所有的国际舞台上展开持续有效的竞争，特别是在整体军事平衡方面以及我们认为的重点战略地区内，更应如此。"
> ——《美国国家安全决策指令第 75 号》，1983 年

作者生平

保罗·肯尼迪 1945 年出生于英格兰北方城市纽卡斯尔的一个普通工薪家庭。在一次接受英国《卫报》采访时，肯尼迪说，家人都以为他中学毕业后就会开始工作。[1] 但令家人没有料到的是，中学毕业后，他考入了纽卡斯尔大学继续学习，专业为历史学；大学毕业后，他又考入牛津大学圣安东尼学院＊（该学院只招收研究生，其中美国学生占多数）继续攻读博士学位，师从英国军事史学家和战略大师巴兹尔·利德尔·哈特＊爵士。

成长于大英帝国末年的肯尼迪总想写一些关于"大国"的东西，尤其是帝国过度扩张方面的历史。年轻时，肯尼迪总是梦想着能为大英帝国服务，但"到我上大学的时候（1963 年），几乎所有帝国的殖民地都已经独立建国"。[2] 欧洲的一个小岛国居然能统治世界四分之一的地方，这可是一件非比寻常的事情。于是，肯尼迪决定要对这样的"大国"现象进行一番深入研究。[3]1982 年，英国和阿根廷就南大西洋只有几千人口的福克兰群岛归属问题发生了军事冲突。虽然英国人最终在这场"马岛战争"＊中获胜，但冲突还是反映了英国在控制海外领地方面的颓势。

肯尼迪凭借其学术造诣在美国耶鲁大学谋得了教职。就职耶鲁大学期间，他出版了《大国的兴衰》一书，并凭借此书成了学术界的超级明星。不久之后，他又被联合国和美国政府聘为顾问。肯尼迪结合自己担任联合国顾问的经历，出版了另一部力作《人类议会》，谈及了联合国的作用、面临的问题和未来的潜力。[4] 从帝国治理到全球管理，肯尼迪的创作涉及了他认为当今世界面临的各种重大问题。

创作背景

第二次世界大战*结束后的近五十年时间里，冷战成了国际政治的主旋律。资本主义*国家美国与共产主义国家苏联之间的关系一度极为紧张。（资本主义是西方世界主流的社会经济制度，其特点为工业私有化；共产主义是一种政治意识形态，强调财产公有化，构成生产方式的生产工具和生产资料均由国家统一管理。）

冷战虽然并未造成直接冲突，但却引发了代理人战争。比如，在朝鲜战争*（1950—1953）和越南战争*（1955—1975）中，美国就是在间接地与中国和苏联作战。此外，冷战期间还发生了一些几乎令大战一触即发的事件，如1962年古巴导弹危机*事件，苏联在古巴部署导弹的企图差点引发一场全面的核大战。简而言之，苏联人和美国人都将对方视为了自己潜在的威胁，整个世界一度笼罩在核毁灭的阴影之下。

肯尼迪原本计划于1986年出版《大国的兴衰》。如果是那样的话，书中所涉及的内容就只有第二次世界大战结束前的大国兴衰史。[5] 但肯尼迪当时已经"开始关注起了美苏两国于20世纪80年代末实施的不平衡的财政政策和巨额的军费开支情况",他意识到要在他的书中对当时的形势有所交代。因此,他将出书计划推迟了一年。[6]

肯尼迪所提到的财政失衡主要是美国政府推行"里根主义"(以美国总统罗纳德·里根*的名字命名的一种战略思想,旨在不断给苏联施加压力)的结果。罗纳德·里根属于意识形态斗争的强硬派,他把苏联称为"邪恶帝国",呼吁美国进行大规模的军备建设。此外,他还以提供武器、资金和培训的方式加大了对反苏维埃组织的支持,支持他们在全球范围内推翻共产主义政府的图谋。[7]

美国为实现这些战略目标,只是增加了少量财政投入,却让苏联原本已显出疲态的国民经济更加恶化。[8]为了和美国相抗衡,苏联不断增加军事投入,甚至达到了整个国民收入的四分之一,这样的状况似乎不太可能再持续下去了。[9]美国在不断增加海外投入,而苏联则开始摇摇欲坠,肯尼迪在这样一个特殊时期撰写了大国政治的历史。

从某种意义上讲,肯尼迪总结得出的16世纪历史发展的模式在他出版该书的时代仍然适用。肯尼迪预言,任何大国在覆灭的过程中都会经历动荡和骚乱。但《大国的兴衰》出版仅仅四年后,在经济和军事上都已不堪重负的苏联竟然解体了,冷战也于1991年以和平的方式迅速走到了终点。这样的结果完全出乎肯尼迪的预料,因为他认为大国的衰落一定会伴有军事冲突,是一个新兴大国击败衰落大国的过程。

1. 约翰·克雷斯："保罗·肯尼迪：新保守派的噩梦"，《卫报》，2008 年 2 月 5 日，登录日期 2015 年 9 月 3 日，http://www.theguardian.com/education/2008/feb/05/academicexperts.highereducationprofile。

2. 保罗·肯尼迪："帝国思想：历史学家的帝国方式教育"，《大西洋月刊》，2008 年 1 月，登录日期 2015 年 9 月 3 日，http://www.theatlantic.com/magazine/archive/2008/01/the-imperial-mind/306566/。

3. 肯尼迪："帝国思想"。

4. 赫·理查兹："重画大图景"，《泰晤士高等教育》，2008 年 8 月 28 日，登录日期 2015 年 9 月 2 日，https://www.timeshighereducation.co.uk/features/redrawing-the-big-picture/403290.article。

5. 克雷斯："保罗·肯尼迪"。

6. 克雷斯："保罗·肯尼迪"。

7. 雷蒙德·L. 加索夫：《伟大的过渡：美苏关系与冷战结束》，华盛顿特区：布鲁金斯学会出版社，1994 年，第 8—9 页。

8. 加索夫：《伟大的过渡》，第 78 页。

9. 沃尔特·拉费伯尔：《美国、俄国和冷战 1945—2002》，纽约：麦格劳-希尔出版社，2002 年，第 335 页。

2 学术背景

要点 🔑

- 国际史研究通过对过去事件模式的分析来解释当今的国际形势。

- 传统的外交史研究关注的是伟大人物和重大事件本身,但现代历史研究关注的则是重大事件的发生模式;重大历史事件一定有其发生的原因,需要解读。

- 肯尼迪关注的是建立大国关系的经济基础,他的研究也反映了他在牛津大学的两位导师——英国历史学家 A. J. P. 泰勒 * 和约翰·加拉格尔 * 的部分研究成果。

著作语境

保罗·肯尼迪的著作《大国的兴衰》(1987)属于国际史研究范畴。传统的国际史研究关注的是伟大人物和国家之间的外交关系,并对这样的研究对象做出解释。但像肯尼迪这样的现代派国际史研究者关注的则是历史的发生模式,并用这些模式去解释当今的世界形势。1789 年,18 世纪的德国历史学家弗里德里希·席勒 * 就曾提出过该学科的研究目的。他认为,国际史学家"必须从大量的事件中选出那些容易理解的,但又在本质上影响和决定了当今世界形势和当代人生活状况的事件"。[1]

我们也必须将《大国的兴衰》置于国际关系 * 领域进行研究。1920 年,曾经是历史研究分支的国际关系研究成了一门独立学科,其标志性事件就是威尔士亚伯大学 * 国际关系学院的成立。国际关系学科试图解释的不是过去所发生事件的模式,而是"为什么国际事件会以既有的方式发生"。[2] 因此，国际关系研究偏向于提出关于国家行为的一般理论，而国际史研究则偏向于解释跨越国界的历史发展趋势。但事实上，两个学科之间并没有明确的分界线，其共同之处多于不同之处。

> "回顾过去，许多人都有罪，没有清白无辜之人。政治活动的目的就是谋求和平与繁荣；但在这一点上，所有政治家最终都失败了，失败的理由各不相同。这是一个没有英雄的故事，也许连反面人物也没有。"
>
> —— A.J.P. 泰勒：《第二次世界大战的起源》

学科概览

19 世纪，外交行为在欧洲日益"专业化"起来。同时，历史研究也越来越关注外交政策和大国政治了。[3]19 世纪的德国学者利奥波德·冯·兰克* 可能要算是第一位现代外交史学家了。他提出了"外交政策*优先"的政治观点，并尝试从国家之间的关系去解释欧洲史。在他看来，为了抵御别国的威胁，各国都在"调用国内各种资源以自保"。[4] 兰克一生著述颇丰，其中就包括著名的《拉丁与条顿民族史》(1824)，[5] 他擅长剖析历史上处于各大巨头统治之下的不同民族之间所发生冲突的长期根源。兰克著作的最大亮点是用"真实数据"（尤其在外交史料方面）将事件真实地呈现在读者面前。

兰克的这种研究方法一直持续到 20 世纪中叶，当时学者的研究重心已开始发生转变。他们不再通过描述历史巨头戏剧性的决定以及其彼此间的关系来讲述历史了，而是开始关注普通大众的行为，探究决定历史的潜在因素。著名的法国历史学家费尔南·布罗代尔*于 1949 年出版了《地中海与腓力二世*时代的地中海世界》一书，这标志着历史研究转向"社会"史学。

布罗代尔研究的是 16 世纪的欧洲，但他关注的重点并不是"历史巨头"们（国王和将军）深思熟虑的外交策略，而是着眼于"长时段"*——缓慢的变化。布罗代尔在地理分界、科技发展和经济事务等问题中发现了决定历史缓慢演变的一些因素。布罗代尔写道，"重大事件通常是突然爆发的"，但想要明白为什么会发生这样的事件，就需要研究那个时代潜在的"更大的运动"[6]。长时段历史研究不会将外交行为视为解释历史事件的工具，而是将其视为需要用潜在因素解释的事实之一。

费尔南·布罗代尔是年鉴学派*的代表人物，他们的研究主要关注的是"长时段"历史，即经济发展与历史事件的关系；20 世纪美国学者伊曼纽尔·沃勒斯坦*则提出了世界体系论*，旨在揭示资本主义经济和社会制度是何以成为单一国际体系之根源的。沃勒斯坦写道："15 世纪末 16 世纪初，当资本主义开始扎根并不断扩张时，出现了我们可称之为'欧洲世界经济体'的体系。"[7]这一世界经济体将劳动进行了全球性分工：欧洲和北美等"核心"国家生产高附加值产品，他们榨取了南半球那些"边缘化"的殖民地或受压迫国家的廉价劳动力和原材料。沃勒斯坦认为，"资本主义就是一种经济模式，这种模式可以让各种经济因素在一个较大的舞台上运行自如，而任何政治实体都无法完全控制如此之大的舞台"，这就使"世界体系在经济上不断扩张"成为可能。[8]

学术渊源

肯尼迪在牛津大学的两位导师 A. J. P. 泰勒和约翰·加拉格尔都是研究英国长期外交史的历史学家。泰勒 1954 年出版的《欧洲霸权之争：1848—1918》探讨了引发第一次世界大战 * 的外交和经济根源。在该书的序言部分，作者通过对不同大国在劳动力、煤炭产量和钢铁产量等具体数据上的对比分析，估算出了各大国的真正实力。[9] 泰勒指出："欧洲的政治家更看重政治现象而不是具体的经济情况。"[10] 但泰勒对 19 世纪强权政治的评价主要是基于强权国家的外交政策。比如，他认为引发第一次世界大战的是德国领导人的野心，而不是某种潜在的物质因素。

肯尼迪在牛津大学读书时的另一位学术导师是历史学家约翰·加拉格尔，他与其他学者于 1961 年合作撰写的一部关于大英帝国时期非洲的专著奠定了他的学术地位。这本《非洲与维多利亚时代：帝国主义的官方思想》读起来更像是在进行理论探讨，而非历史讲述。正如加拉格尔本人所说："我们没打算写 19 世纪非洲地区的历史，但研究非洲是我们提出有关民族主义和世界政治理论假设的基础。"[11] 我们再次看到了经济至关重要的作用："源自欧洲的经济动力"将外国的地区也融为了欧洲的"市场和投资地"。安全则是第二重要的动因，在与对手的扩张大战中，各个大国都想通过扩大自己在海外的领地来抢得先机。[12]

需要指出的是，加拉格尔和沃勒斯坦在某些重要方面的观点是存在分歧的。加拉格尔认为，各个国家为了巩固其海外事业是独自进行海外领地扩张的；沃勒斯坦则认为，所有国家都是在一个超国家的经济体系下按经济规律运作的，每个国家只是整个体系的一分子。

1. 弗里德里希·席勒：转引自高尔登·A.克雷格，"史学家与国际关系研究"，《美国历史评论》第 88 卷，1983 年第 1 期，第 3 页。

2. 托布琼·克努森：《国际关系史理论》，曼彻斯特：曼彻斯特大学出版社，1997 年，第 6 页。

3. 帕特里克·芬尼："国际史概述"，载《帕尔格雷夫国际史前沿》，帕特里克·芬尼编，贝辛斯托克：帕尔格雷夫–麦克米兰出版社，2005 年，第 1 页。

4. 西奥多·H.冯·劳厄：《利奥波德·兰克：形成时期》，新泽西州普林斯顿：普林斯顿大学出版社，1950 年，第 167 页。

5. 利奥波德·冯·兰克：《拉丁与条顿民族史 1494—1514》，G.R.丹尼斯译，伦敦：乔治贝尔父子出版社，1909 年。

6. 费尔南·布罗代尔：《地中海与腓力二世时代的地中海世界》，西恩·雷诺兹译，纽约：哈珀与罗出版社，1972 年，第 21 页。

7. 伊曼纽尔·沃勒斯坦：《现代世界体系 I：16 世纪资本主义农业和欧洲世界经济起源（新序言版）》，伯克利：加利福尼亚大学出版社，2011 年，第 15 页。

8. 沃勒斯坦：《现代世界体系》，第 348 页。

9. A.J.P.泰勒：《欧洲霸权之争：1848—1918》，牛津：牛津大学出版社，1969 年，第 xxvi—xxxiv 页。

10. 泰勒：《欧洲霸权之争》，第 xxxii 页。

11. 罗纳德·罗宾逊等：《非洲与维多利亚时代：帝国主义的官方思想》，贝辛斯托克：麦克米兰出版社，1981 年，第 xxv 页。

12. 罗宾逊等：《非洲与维多利亚时代》，第 485 页。

3 主导命题

要点 🔑

- 学者们关注的问题：在研究超级大国的政治时，哪些因素可以用来解释总的历史发展模式？

- 两种主导研究方法：国际关系学派强调结构因素的作用；"伟人"研究学派强调个人决策的作用。

- 与同时代的学者相比，肯尼迪研究的是较长时间跨度的历史，他既关注结构因素的作用，**也**关注个人决策的作用。

核心问题

保罗·肯尼迪在《大国的兴衰》（1987）一书中所探讨的问题与政治理论家及历史学家多年来一直在思考的一个问题高度相关，即决定政治格局的本质因素是什么？

年鉴学派的学者主张长时段研究法，即以较长时间段内的历史（通常就是社会）变化为研究对象。以这种方法对政治事件进行解释并提出治国理政方略的理论研究已经开展了一百多年。理论家希望找到决定历史的内在因素，以便预测未来，而历史学家则希望借此对过去所发生的事件做出解释。

然而，美国与苏联及其盟友的核对峙已将冷战推向了危险的境地，解决这一重大问题比以往任何时候都显得刻不容缓。在双方都拥有核武器的情况下，预测这一紧张时期的未来走势实质上就是在预测一个生死存亡的问题。这就迫切需要学者和政治家们能结合历史经验对当前形势做出准确的判断，这也正是国际关系这一学科从一开始就秉持的研究宗旨。

再者，到第二次世界大战结束时，大国之间的相互依赖程度已比过去密切了许多。在肯尼迪看来，像美、苏、中、日等大国和欧共体都应该合理行使和管控自己的经济权和军事权，这样就不会发生权力滥用的情况，也就不会为自己播下衰落的种子了。[1]

> "任何人只要花点时间去学习历史就会知道，创造和编纂历史的人总会做出一些不好的预言来。"
>
> —— 约翰·刘易斯·加迪斯："长久安定"

参与者

20 世纪美国政治学家肯尼思·华尔兹 * 对大国政治的研究源自不同的视角。他于 1979 年出版了专著《国际政治理论》，描绘了一幅完全由理论构建出来的（非历史观的）全球政治图景。他认为，个别国家的个别特殊行为在整个历史进程中完全是偶发性的。毕竟，战争永远都是大国关系变化带来的结果，无论国家的管理方式如何，也无论其管理者是谁。[2] 华尔兹的理论核心是：国际社会是无人管治的，处于无政府状态 * 的，因此每个国家自己必须负责自身的安全。从这个意义上讲，所有国家都有相同的利益（即生存）和确保利益的手段（即军事）。[3] 我们只能依据各国的实力对它们进行比较。

华尔兹常常把国家比作台球。他认为，不同台球的差别体现在尺寸大小和重量上，而不同国家的区别体现在物质能量上。因此，历史就是对权力平衡结果的详细描述。华尔兹用自己的理论对 20 世纪 70 年代的世界局势做了判断，认为相互敌对的美、苏两国绝对不会开战，因为那样做的风险太高了。虽然两国都很强大，但它们都不具备彻底压倒对方的优势。研究国际关系的学者把这种状态称为稳定的两极关系 *。

肯尼迪在耶鲁大学的同事——美国历史学家约翰·刘易斯·加迪斯 * 则表达了不同的观点。在加迪斯看来，"如果两极关系的结构自身能确保稳定的话，那么美苏双边关系的某些本质特征也应能实现这种目的"。[4] 在维持稳定方面，起作用的不仅有势力均衡的状态，还有身处其中的当事者。加迪斯试图解释为什么美苏之间在关系并不友好的情况下还能保持稳定的关系。他认为，超级大国 *（在政治、军事和经济上占主导地位的国家）只要能遵循如下的行为模式就可以维持彼此间的和平：

- 尊重彼此的势力范围 *（行使特殊权力的地区），

- 避免军事冲突，

- 避免核对抗，

- 接受可以预料到的不公正之事（即不会令人感到震惊或引起强烈反应的不公正之事，比如，可以接受政治犯存在的事实），

- 避免干涉他国内政。[5]

加迪斯在解释历史"稳定"这一结果时，分析的是超级大国所做的决策，而非其自身的性质。

当时的论战

肯尼迪的探索路径在他所处的时代是独具匠心的。他从不直接评论华尔兹或加迪斯的历史观。概括来讲，肯尼迪与华尔兹的不同之处在于他的研究对象为特定问题，而他与加迪斯的不同之处在于他的研究目的是寻找普适性的解释："正因为没有经济史学家和军

事史学家进入该研究领域，（关于大国辉煌历史的）故事才没有得到人们的深入挖掘。"[6]

肯尼迪指出，国际关系研究和历史研究（包括所谓的"大"历史研究）仅用单一因素去解释整个人类史就会出现研究方法上的以偏概全。这归根结底是没有将大国现象放到一段**较长时期的**历史视域下去考虑。加迪斯关注的只是某一特定大国或大国集团；华尔兹关注的是广义的权力概念。肯尼迪说："大多数读者和听众想得到的是**更**详尽和**更**深入的背景挖掘，因为这方面的研究鲜有人做。"[7]

肯尼迪喜欢引用 19 世纪德国政治家奥托·冯·俾斯麦＊所说过的一句话："所有这些大国都行走在'时代的潮流'中，他们虽然'既不能创造，也无法控制'这样的潮流，但却可以'凭借多多少少的驾驶技巧和经验'航行其上。"[8]肯尼迪的理论弥补了国际关系研究和历史研究之间的空白。

---

1. 保罗·肯尼迪：《大国的兴衰》，纽约：温特吉出版社，1989 年，第 540 页。
2. 肯尼思·华尔兹：《国际政治理论》，雷丁：艾迪森-维斯利出版社，1979 年，第 65 页。
3. 华尔兹：《国际政治理论》，第 99 页。
4. 约翰·刘易斯·加迪斯："长久安定：战后国际体系的稳定因素"，《国际安全》第 10 卷，1986 年第 4 期，第 110 页。
5. 加迪斯："长久安定"，第 133—138 页。
6. 肯尼迪：《大国的兴衰》，第 xxv 页。
7. 肯尼迪：《大国的兴衰》，第 xxv 页。
8. 肯尼迪：《大国的兴衰》，第 540 页。

4 作者贡献

要点 🔑

- 肯尼迪希望能将 16 世纪至 20 世纪末欧洲大国的历史呈现给读者。

- 他对公元 1500 年之后的政治资料和经济数据进行了整理和分析，但他有意不做预测，也无意创立任何理论。

- 《大国的兴衰》的创作思想源自德国历史学家奥斯瓦德·施本格勒 * 和加拿大裔美国历史学家威廉·麦克尼尔 * 的学术争鸣。这两位历史学家虽生于不同年代，但他们对西方世界的未来都有过精辟的论述。

作者目标

保罗·肯尼迪在《大国的兴衰》一开篇就说明了其创作的大概意图。他说他想从权力、影响力以及全球地位三方面谈起，"追踪并解释过去的五个世纪里欧洲相互关联的各个大国的兴衰存亡史"。[1]

为什么时长为五个世纪？为什么范围只限于欧洲？毕竟，这个时间段之外也有大国存在，比如罗马帝国 *。另外，欧洲之外也有大国存在，比如中国的明王朝 *（1368—1644）。但肯尼迪并没有去考虑这些问题。他解释说，选择从公元 1500 年开始，是因为 1500 年标志着"跨大洋全球国家体系"的开始；选择重点研究欧洲，是因为决定跨大洋全球国家体系运作方式的正是欧洲大陆上的国家。[2]

肯尼迪喜欢用欧洲的独特地理位置这一特征去解释为什么欧洲最终会成为政治意义上的"世界中心"。不同的河流、山脉和森林将欧洲的领土分割了开来，形成了许多自然的权力中心，这些中心独霸一方，相互争斗，都想占据霸主的地位。在这种竞争体系中，只有那些最能战斗和最善统治的中心才能最终胜出。[3]

军事实力虽不是唯一的决定因素，但无疑是最重要的因素。1492 年，意大利探险家哥伦布 * 远航探险成功后，海外征服就成了一项可能的事业，欧洲也因此在物质上赶超了世界上的其他地区。统治西班牙和奥地利的哈布斯堡家族欲夺欧洲霸主之位，其他欧洲国家则联合起来同哈布斯堡家族断断续续地斗争了 150 年，最终击碎了哈布斯堡家族的梦想。[4] 需要指出的是，哈布斯堡王朝并非一个国家，而是一个家族联盟，该家族联盟通过世袭制统治着欧洲一大片动荡不定的地区。然而，无论是为了国家利益还是家族利益，无论是为了领土扩张还是精忠报国，只要有流血牺牲的战争发生，一定会付出人口减少和经济衰退的代价。

> "与政治学家不同，历史学家发现过去的证据几乎总是变动不居的，因此无法从普遍的理论中得出不容怀疑的科学结论来。"
>
> —— 保罗·肯尼迪：《大国的兴衰》

研究方法

肯尼迪收集了大量的信息，并用多种方法手段进行了分析。《大国的兴衰》"很多部分在描述战争……但从严格意义上讲，这并不是一本有关军事史的著作"。同样，该书虽然讲到了全球经济的演化过程，但"也不是一部有关经济史的著作"。[5] 作者是将政治家行为和经济因素综合在一起来分析历史进程的。

肯尼迪指出，他是通过分析经济和技术的缓慢变化来解释大国政治的。因而，历史学家可能会认为该书的内容"虽宽泛但又不失详尽"。而政治学家则会将该书视为作者在尝试提出的一种理论，即我们可以通过观察大国的经济走势来预测其未来的表现。但事实上肯尼迪并没有那样做，他的初衷并不是要提出预测性的理论，而只是想"看懂"历史事件。肯尼迪的观点可简单总结如下：财富不一定代表成功，但"在过去五百年间，与那些的国家的统治地位相呼应的恰恰是其领先于其他国家的经济水平"。肯尼迪认为如何用这一观点去预测未来也许值得我们思考——但他自己却不愿这样做，也不愿去下精确的、科学式的论断。[6]

时代贡献

尝试写有关西方"大"历史的不只有肯尼迪一人。1922年，德国历史学家奥斯瓦德·施本格勒在其专著《西方的衰落》中曾问过这样一个问题："历史有其自身的逻辑吗？"[7]他认为我们应该用"文化"（比如西方文化）来分析历史，还应该视文化为有生命周期的东西，正如自然界中的生物有从生到死的生命周期一样。施本格勒用代表某社会主要精神的"基本符号"来定义文化。在他看来，代表西方文化的"符号"就是浮士德精神。浮士德*是德国民间传说中至少可追溯至16世纪的人物。在传说中，浮士德把自己的灵魂卖给了魔鬼，换回了无限的知识。西方社会是"浮士德式"的社会，因为人类已将自己的灵魂和土地出卖，换回的是高精技术和工业生产。随着时间的推移，文化在慢慢发展为文明的过程中会越来越倾向于向外扩张。施本格勒认为，文明终将会走向衰落，因为在文明形成的那一刻，文化就停止了创新，转而开始向外扩张。

20 世纪加拿大裔美国历史学家威廉·麦克尼尔不认同施本格勒悲观的周期论观点。他在 1962 年出版的《西方的兴起》一书中强调，我们不应把历史视为不同文化都要经历的一系列轮回事件。相反，"与拥有全新技术的文化接触才是推动社会发生重大历史变革的主因"。他认为，人类文明，尤其是西方文明，就是各种先进技术的结晶。[8] 不同文明是相互分离的，但彼此的交流决定了其生命周期。

麦克尼尔与施本格勒的观点几乎完全相反，他认为，西方在掌握了航海技术之时就奠定了其在全球的统治地位。这也让欧洲国家可以开始向外无限扩张："结果就是将大西洋东岸的欧洲与全球大部分的海岸连接了起来。"欧洲成了"赢家"，因为它拥有了先进的技术，可以很好地利用其他地区的一切资源。[9]

施本格勒和麦克尼尔二人关注的都是西方与其他地区的相对地位关系，他们所讲述的西方"兴衰"故事与肯尼迪的讲述也非常相似。但是，肯尼迪的研究无疑吸收了更多学者的思想，强调了技术和地理等诸多因素在大国兴衰过程中的作用。

---

1. 保罗·肯尼迪：《大国的兴衰》，纽约：温特吉出版社，1989 年，第 xv 页。
2. 肯尼迪：《大国的兴衰》，第 xv 页。
3. 肯尼迪：《大国的兴衰》，第 30 页。
4. 肯尼迪：《大国的兴衰》，第 31 页。
5. 肯尼迪：《大国的兴衰》，第 xv 页。
6. 肯尼迪：《大国的兴衰》，第 xxiv 页。

7. 奥斯瓦德·施本格勒：《西方的衰落》，赫尔穆德·华纳编，查尔斯·F. 阿特金森译，牛津：牛津大学出版社，1991年，第3页。

8. 威廉·麦克尼尔："二十五年后再评《西方的兴起》"，《世界史杂志》第1卷，1990年第1期，第2页。

9. 威廉·麦克尼尔：《西方的兴起：人类共同体史》，芝加哥：芝加哥大学出版社，第1991年，第564—565页。

第二部分：学术思想

5 思想主脉

要点 🔑

- 尽管没有学者给"大国"下过正式的定义，但这一术语通常用来指那些能在军事竞争中与其他任何国家相抗衡的国家。
- 当大国的军事投入超出其生产力水平时，就会走向衰落。当大国的军事实力与生产力水平领先于其他国家后，它就会慢慢崛起。
- 《大国的兴衰》一书中虽然没有复杂的数学或学术方面的专用行话，但它的长度足以吓退一些读者。

核心主题

保罗·肯尼迪写《大国的兴衰》一书的主要目的是要回答这样一个问题：一个什么样的国家能被称为"大国"？我们可以从两个方面来给"大国"下个定义。简而言之，大国就是指在战争中能击败其他任何对手的国家；从社会交往角度讲，大国就是被其他国家认为强大的国家。因此，一个国家的"大国"地位有赖于其他国家的承认，而不在于它是否达到了某个任意制定出来的标准。

肯尼迪书中一开始关注的"大国"是以西班牙、法兰西和奥地利为政治中心的家族王朝。写到后半部分时，肯尼迪关注起了"大国俱乐部"中的新晋成员——俄国、英国和德国等国家。

在肯尼迪看来，"世界军事力量平衡（即主权国家间的相对均势）中所有的重大改变追根溯源都是因为在生产力平衡上先发生了某些变化"。[1] 他的结论似乎是：谁拥有了财富，谁就拥有了胜利。但事情远非如此简单，大国即便占尽了资源优势，也是会犯错误的。更为常见的情况是，两个大国之间的血腥冲突会持续相当长的时间，虽然胜利通常属于经济实力更为强大的一方。

> "第一次世界大战的结果事先就能预料到……虽然这种说法非常不妥当……但这里所列的证据表明，整个战争的进程（从双方最初的僵持，到意大利'鸡肋式'的加入，到俄国实力慢慢耗尽，再到美国的果断干预……）与经济发展和工业生产水平密切相关，与不同阶段各盟国能否有效动员兵力密切相关。"
>
> —— 保罗·肯尼迪：《大国的兴衰》

思想探索

肯尼迪首先谈论的是哈布斯堡王朝的"兴衰"，即发生于1516年到1689年间的故事。1516年，哈布斯堡家族的查理成功加冕为西班牙国王，史称卡洛斯一世。但按先辈的惯例，卡洛斯一世同时也是查理五世*，即神圣罗马帝国*的皇帝。神圣罗马帝国是当时的一个政治实体，其势力范围包括奥地利大部、尼德兰、那不勒斯以及欧洲周边的其他一些地区。但这个"帝国"不是一个中央集权制的国家，而是哈布斯堡家族统治下的一个诸侯联合体。

在谈到哈布斯堡王朝衰败的原因时，肯尼迪认为，尽管哈布斯堡家族在欧洲和新世界（西班牙在南美洲的殖民地）拥有巨额财富，但仍然无法负担一百四十多年来多线作战的开销。他们不断建造战舰投入战斗，却不使用商船进行贸易，还在内外贸易上设置重重壁垒，并且大肆驱逐犹太人出境。[2] 简言之，哈布斯堡家族"没有认识到维护强大军事机器的经济基础有多么重要"。

肯尼迪由此总结出了非常重要的经验："工人农民和军官士兵一样重要。"[3] 一个国家只有维持较高的生产力水平才能保证其在军事方面的投入和作为。

哈布斯堡王朝就这样因忽视经济问题而走向了衰落。不久之后，又有大不列颠、奥匈帝国（没落后的哈布斯堡帝国）、普鲁士（今日德国北部地区）、法兰西和俄罗斯等五国登上了大国的舞台。当时，这些欧洲列强都在斥资建设自己的常备军队，肯尼迪将这一现象称之为"军事革命"。[4]

肯尼迪写道，地理和财政因素也同等重要。[5] 和平时期维持军队的运转需要国家财政的支持。各大国还须考虑侵略者会从哪些可能的地理战线向自己发起进攻。在这种情况下，那些彼此争斗并投入巨资，力争成为"大国"的国家便进入了疯狂的发展阶段，它们将大量的资金投向了为军队提供住所、装备和训练的产业。

历史学家约翰·布鲁尔*将这种现象称为"财政—军事国家"，并总结出了如下特点："高额的税收，不断发展、有序的民政管理，常备军，以及成为大国的决心。"[6] 从根本上讲，强大的财政支持就是强大军事实力的保证。正如肯尼迪所言，战场上出现失策并不可怕，可怕的是"在人员培训、物资供应、组织保障和经济基础方面失去了优势"。[7]

肯尼迪对历史的剖析就是本着这样的逻辑。正如他在评论第一次世界大战（1914—1918）时所指出的那样，美国于 1917 年加入战争之后，获胜方的大国就"在生产力方面拥有了明显的优势"。当然，这种"明显的优势"不仅体现在占有资源的数量上，还体现在资源的合理配置上。

肯尼迪还讨论了德国的兴登堡计划*，即加倍生产军火的计划。

在新兴工业资源领域，德国进行了"大规模基础设施投资"，其中就包括建设武器制造专用的鼓风炉。不过，要实现这一目标，国家需要对所有熟练工人重新做出调整，并且可能会长期忽视其他的工农业生产。[8] 最后，德国因忽视经济多样性而遭受的损失并不亚于外部军事力量破坏所带来的损失。

同理，肯尼迪对二战的结局也给出了同样的解释。"中等强国"（英、法、德）既需维持其帝国疆域，又得应付旷日持久的战争，最终精疲力竭，不可避免地走上了衰落的老路。[9] 只有美国和苏联成了主宰世界的两个相互制约的超级大国。

语言表述

先不说《大国的兴衰》一书的字数，光是书中讨论的话题就能吓退一些读者，但肯尼迪在书中的语言表述却是清晰流畅的，没有艰深晦涩的术语。他喜欢用图表来支持自己的论证，比如，1940年至1943年间军备开销情况的比较以及二战中交战双方的开支比较等。因为文本内容有简单的图表作补充，读者是不需要做任何数学运算的。[10]

肯尼迪是按时间顺序讲述历史事件的，书中大部分内容是在概述各种军事行为（包括长达百年的战争）以及经济与技术的发展情况。这些事实其实就是我们试图要解释的历史事件。

最后，肯尼迪在附录中提供了许多例子和详尽的解释。读者还可以根据每章的尾注更好地理解该章的内容，作者在注释中不仅引用了许多历史人物的解释性言论，还列出了许多有价值的参考书目。

1. 保罗·肯尼迪:《大国的兴衰》,纽约:温特吉出版社,1989 年,第 439 页。

2. 肯尼迪:《大国的兴衰》,第 55 页。

3. 肯尼迪:《大国的兴衰》,第 72 页。

4. M. 罗伯茨:"军事革命 1560—1600",载《瑞典史论文集》,M.罗伯茨编,伦敦:韦登菲尔德-尼科尔森出版社,1967 年,第 217 页。

5. 肯尼迪:《大国的兴衰》,第 76 页。

6. 约翰·布鲁尔:《大国筋骨:战争、金钱与英格兰 1688—1783》,伦敦:世纪哈钦森出版社,1988 年,第 137 页。

7. 肯尼迪:《大国的兴衰》,第 192 页。

8. 肯尼迪:《大国的兴衰》,第 270 页。

9. 肯尼迪:《大国的兴衰》,第 366—367 页。

10. 肯尼迪:《大国的兴衰》,第 335 页。

6 思想支脉

要点 ⚷━

- 16 世纪至 20 世纪大国之间的动态平衡为 20 世纪下半叶的新一轮竞争搭好了舞台。

- 冷战是美苏领导的世界两极对峙的结果，共产主义和资本主义意识形态相互竞争，世界面临核战争威胁；但冷战的深层动因仍是经济利益。

- 肯尼迪认为美国正处于衰落期，理由是其全球性投入已远超其实际承受能力；但并非所有评论家都接受这一观点。

其他思想

在《大国的兴衰》一书中，保罗·肯尼迪从国际视角考察了大国权力平衡的动态变化。更为重要的是，他还分析了 20 世纪国际体系形成的根源。该书的第二个主要观点是：经济发展的不平衡对现代国家体系的形成"产生了长期的、至关重要的影响"。[1]

20 世纪的国家体系是两次世界大战的结果，而两次世界大战本身则是 18 世纪和 19 世纪五大强国争夺霸权的结果。"（二战结束后，）全球的权力平衡变得清晰了起来……与之前的状况已完全不同。"[2] 法国、意大利和德国在经历战争后实力大减；第一个非欧洲大国日本也失去了其统领亚洲的绝对实力。英国虽然比邻国恢复得相对快一些，但也无法与新崛起的美、苏两大强国相抗衡。

除了分析形成欧洲多极 * 国际体系（有许多国家参与争夺霸权的体系）的根源和动因外，肯尼迪还探讨了 1945 年至 1991 年间的两极国际体系（两个国家争夺主导权的体系）是如何形成的。不过，肯尼迪最感兴趣的还是探讨美国的走向问题。他指出，在1945年至1991年与苏联的冷战和之后的两极竞争中的美国也会陷入历史发展的老路，并逐渐走向衰落。

> "当时只有美国才有足够的生产和技术资源，不仅能发动两次大规模的常规战争，还投入了科学家、原材料和资金（约20亿美元）去研制原子弹这种不知能否发挥作用的新型武器。随后，广岛遭到美国的原子弹轰炸，柏林被苏联红军攻陷，这不仅意味着另一场战争的结束，也标志着世界新秩序的开始。"
>
> —— 保罗·肯尼迪：《大国的兴衰》

思想探究

1945年第二次世界大战结束后，苏、美两国在欧洲形成了对峙的局面。苏共（苏联最高权力机关）总书记约瑟夫·斯大林*巩固了其控制东欧的地位。在"保持高度军事安全……防止未来侵略者"的同时，斯大林还命令军队进驻中亚，以防苏联未来的征服之地被纳入美国的势力范围。[3] 而美国则试图在全球推广所谓的"美式和平"*。该术语指的是美国统治下的和平与繁荣，但却无法掩盖南半球发展中国家存在许多内部暴乱的事实。肯尼迪认为这一术语是在模仿19世纪末的"英式和平"*，当时英国的"生产力水平和世界影响力"在世界上占据了主导地位，世界也处于相对稳定的时期。[4] 但是，意识形态较量和核武器威慑使20世纪大国之间的全球性竞争发生了根本性的变化。

两大阵营都坚持自己的意识形态。美国及其盟友拥护资本主义制度（该制度提倡个人自由，重视选举，突出工业和资源的私有化）；苏联及其盟友则推行共产主义制度（该制度要求公民服从国家意志，国家拥有并管理工业及各种资源，强调财产的公有化）。1945年至1953年间任美国总统的哈里·S. 杜鲁门*曾宣称："美国……（帮助）人民维持他们的制度和领土完整，帮助他们反抗企图将极权*政府统治强加于他们的侵略运动。"换言之，杜鲁门立誓要阻止苏联共产主义向新的国家扩张。[5]

早期各国间战争的根源要么是宗教纠纷，要么是抽象的"国家利益"。但冷战时期的敌对双方都从心底里认为当时的国际冲突就是一场全球性的善恶之争。与以往的大国对峙不同，冷战时期因对峙的双方都拥有核武器，整个世界都被牵扯了进来。[6]美国和苏联都拥有轻摁按钮就足以毁灭地球上所有生命的能力。

虽然肯尼迪用了许多修辞性的语言来评述冷战，但他对该时期对立双方冲突的分析与他对历史上大国之间冲突的分析均出自相同的逻辑假设，即冲突归根结底还是工业和经济上的冲突，而不仅仅是军事上的冲突。冷战期间，苏联的军事实力和核威慑力明显与其"经济成就和水平不相称"，在技术创新方面尤其如此。[7]肯尼迪不愿意对未来的国际政治进行预测（如果这样做，他就从历史研究转向了政治理论研究）。但他却反复强调了一点："一个大国在国防、消费和投资方面如果不能做到大致平衡的话，是不可能长期保持其大国地位的。"[8]

被忽视之处

肯尼迪在基本完成本书的写作后，决定再增加几个章节来讨论当今美国的情况。虽然他在新增章节中的论述并不一定与其主要理论相关，但这些章节恰恰是**最**受人们关注的部分，因为按照他前面的理论推演，美国正处于相对的衰落期。当今的美国就像"1600年左右的西班牙帝国或 1900 年左右的大英帝国"一样，必须为过去几十年里所做出的军事承诺而在海外不断投入兵力。[9]

肯尼迪认为，美国可能会面临过度扩张的风险，"华盛顿的决策者们必须面对一个非常尴尬但却一直存在的事实，即美国需要履行保护其全球利益的任务总量已远远超出其实际所能承担的能力范围"。[10] 在肯尼迪看来，当今美国的衰落和 19 世纪英国的衰落简直如出一辙。

肯尼迪指出，**相对**下降的经济表现是这种过度扩张的根源。虽然美国在二战结束时比世界上其他国家的负债都要低，但其国民生产总值*（一个国家所有国民在一年内生产的产品和服务价值的总和）及制造业和农业的总产量都在下降。[11] 而与此同时，美国在海外的投入却在不断增加，越来越大的军费开销让整个国家不堪重负。

评论家虽然并未完全忽视这一观点，但这并不是肯尼迪理论的核心内容。一位早期评论家——美国保守党政治分析人士塞缪尔·亨廷顿*就认为，肯尼迪的过度扩张将导致衰落这一理论有可能是正确的。不过他同时也指出，该理论并不一定适用于美国的情况。因为在他看来，肯尼迪的衰退论太过依赖"经济实力都有相似来源"这一假设了。亨廷顿认为，"美国强大的经济实力的主要来源"包括资本主义市场竞争、社会流动、通过移民和大学不断更新思想文化。亨廷顿认为肯尼迪只是将经济实力简单地等同于诸如粮食产量或工业产值等生产能力了。[12]

1. 保罗·肯尼迪:《大国的兴衰》,纽约:温特吉出版社,1989 年,第 439 页。

2. 肯尼迪:《大国的兴衰》,第 357 页。

3. 肯尼迪:《大国的兴衰》,第 363 页。

4. 肯尼迪:《大国的兴衰》,第 192 页。

5. 肯尼迪:《大国的兴衰》,第 372 页。

6. 肯尼迪:《大国的兴衰》,第 370 页。

7. 肯尼迪:《大国的兴衰》,第 429 页。

8. 肯尼迪:《大国的兴衰》,第 446 页。

9. 肯尼迪:《大国的兴衰》,第 515 页。

10. 肯尼迪:《大国的兴衰》,第 515 页。

11. 肯尼迪:《大国的兴衰》,第 529 页。

12. 塞缪尔·亨廷顿:"美国:衰落还是复兴?",《外交事务》第 67 卷,1988 年第 2 期,第 89 页。

7 历史成就

要点 🔑

- 一些评论家对肯尼迪的经济与国力关系理论提出了质疑；他们认为肯尼迪的研究只关注单一因素，无法解释那些源于其他因素的事实。

- 虽然《大国的兴衰》并未对冷战会如何结束做出预测，但过度扩张无疑起到了一定的影响；美国未来可能会经历与其他大国相似命运的观点引起了人们的关注。

- 评论家认为肯尼迪的分析方法有其局限性，因为他的理论假设只适用于欧洲国家；他们认为肯尼迪用欧洲大国的标准将一些非欧洲的强国排除在了大国之列。

观点评价

有关保罗·肯尼迪所著《大国的兴衰》的一些问题并不太容易回答。比如：该书是否为理解特殊的"大国政治"历史提供了有效的解释模型？它是否能解释（而非预测）为什么历史事件会以特定的方式发生？

虽然澳大利亚学者 J. L. 理查德森 * 认为肯尼迪不愿进行预测是"一种留待学界讨论的、谦虚的做法"，不过他同时也发现肯尼迪的结论确实"简单得令人失望"。他指出，肯尼迪没有解释国家如何形成联盟，他们又是如何分辨敌友的。[1] 其次，尽管他承认肯尼迪在分析经济发展与战争的关系方面做得非常出色，理查德森也指出他完全没必要非得出一个结论不可。理查德森写道，"经济上最强联盟最终获胜"让肯尼迪的结论显得过于简单了。"首先，为什么会形成特定的联盟？为什么重大战争就在那个特定的时间发生，而其他时间却少有战争，甚或完全没有战争呢？……肯尼迪的研究会引发人们提出这样的问题，但对此他几乎没做任何回答。"[2]

实际上，理查德森是在批评肯尼迪只能对已发生过的事件进行解释，却解释不了那些历史上曾经避开过的战争。难道我们的历史就只是"大国政治史"或大国参与的战争史吗？在理查德森看来，肯尼迪的研究在对经济的、战略的、管理的和技术的变化密切关注的同时却过于弱化了政治家对历史的决定性作用，只是将其视为不太重要的"有关分析因素"。[3]

> "冷战结束的结果就是一种国际体系的崩塌，这是现代史上第二次出现这样的事情。"
>
> —— 约翰·刘易斯·加迪斯："国际关系理论与冷战结束"

当时的成就

《大国的兴衰》于 1987 年发表。据肯尼迪在耶鲁大学的同事——著名历史学家约翰·刘易斯·加迪斯所说，该书激发了美国人的民族意识，因为它提出了"大国身份事实上只是个转瞬即逝的现象"这一观点；照此推理，美国的大国地位也只是个暂时现象。[4]此外，肯尼迪还暗示冷战不会以和平的方式结束。加迪斯引用了肯尼迪的结论：帝国的覆灭总是伴随着战争，"那些看到苏联目前深陷困境而欢欣鼓舞甚至盼望它早日覆灭的人们不要忘了，这样的演变通常是以巨大代价换来的"。[5]

但这一次，历史没有重演。冷战结束和苏联解体是在相对和平的环境下发生的。促成欧洲社会主义国家彼此合作的《华沙条约》*于 1989 年正式废止。没有了苏联的支持，东欧那些社会主义国家领导人很快便相继下台。结果，美国变成了唯一的超级大国。

虽然肯尼迪没有预测冷战会**怎样**结束，但他知道冷战终将会结束。一种流行的观点认为，冷战结束似乎确实印证了肯尼迪的理论。罗纳德·里根（1981—1989 年美国总统）增加了国防开支，迫使苏联也不计代价地增加其军费支出。此外，苏联在海外的军事投入也超出了其承受能力。这些因素都导致苏联经济失去了可持续发展的能力。但我们也应注意到，里根在军备上的开销也确实加大了美国的财政赤字（支出与收入之差），而且还削弱了肯尼迪认为非常重要的"生产力基础"。[6]

然而，也有学者并不认同上述对肯尼迪研究的评价。美国政治学家理查德·内德·勒博*和加拿大国际关系专家詹尼斯·格罗斯·斯坦因*就认为，是军备竞赛拉长了冷战的战线。在他们看来，如果美苏两国领导人当时能够面对面交流、彼此充满信任的话，冲突早就结束了。[7]

局限性

英国历史学家杰里米·布莱克*指出了肯尼迪研究工作中的一个问题，即对"大国"如何界定的问题。当然，其他致力于"宏观"研究的西方历史学家也面临着同样的问题。

学者们通常把"大国"定义为在工业和财力方面具有超强实力的国家。但是，一个国家要想加入大国俱乐部，其实力还需得到俱乐部其他成员的认可。布莱克认为，如果这样的话，西方之外的国家就会被排除在大国名单之外。事实上，成为"大国"需要具备的条件完全是以西方国家的特征开列出来的。"因此，20 世纪的日本和中国之所以能被视为大国"，是因为它们具备了西方世界对大国要求的那些条件，"而在这之前，它们都不在大国之列"。[8] 换言之，虽然任何国家都可以进入大国俱乐部玩游戏，但游戏规则是由西方世界制定的。

布莱克认为，如果肯尼迪没有把大国的前提条件预设为欧洲国家的话，那么诸如 13 世纪横跨欧亚大陆的蒙古帝国 * 等欧洲之外的国家也应被视为强国。布莱克提出了衡量大国地位的其他的可能标准，比如荣誉和声望，尽管这些看上去与财政或军事实力没有多少关系。布莱克写道，如果不考虑荣誉的话，"很难解释为什么肯尼迪会将奥地利视为 18 世纪以来的'边缘强国'"，因为奥地利的物质资源相对而言并不富足。[9]

---

1. J. L. 理查德森："保罗·肯尼迪和国际关系理论：与罗伯特·吉尔平的理论比较"，《澳大利亚国际事务杂志》第 45 卷，1991 年第 1 期，第 75 页。

2. 理查德森："保罗·肯尼迪和国际关系理论"，第 76 页。

3. 理查德森："保罗·肯尼迪和国际关系理论"，第 76 页。

4. 约翰·刘易斯·加迪斯："国际关系理论与冷战结束"，《国际安全》第 17 卷，1992 年第 3 期，第 50—51 页。

5. 保罗·肯尼迪：《大国的兴衰》，纽约：温特吉出版社，1989 年，第 514 页。

6. 理查德·内德·勒博和詹尼斯·格罗斯·斯坦因："里根和苏联人"，《大西洋月刊》，1994 年第 2 期，登录日期 2015 年 9 月 12 日，http://www.theatlantic.com/past/politics/foreign/reagrus.htm。

7. 勒博和斯坦因："里根和苏联人"。

8. 杰里米·布莱克:《大国与霸权图谋:1500 年之后的世界秩序》, 伦敦:劳特利奇出版社, 2008 年, 第 1—2 页。

9. 布莱克:《大国与霸权图谋》, 第 20 页。

8 著作地位

要点 🔑

- 《大国的兴衰》是肯尼迪在宏观外交史研究方面的扛鼎之作。
- 肯尼迪起初的研究重心是高级政治学，后来转向了全球治理。
- 《大国的兴衰》因探讨美国衰落问题而为世人所关注；肯尼迪也因此成了一位在学术界有影响力的名人。

定位

《大国的兴衰》不是保罗·肯尼迪的第一部重要著作，甚至也不是他以"兴衰"命名的第一部著作。肯尼迪于1976年出版的第一部重要著作是《英国海上霸权的兴衰》，该书反映了肯尼迪早期对大英帝国如何平衡其海陆军事实力方面的研究兴趣。在随后的研究中，肯尼迪将研究重心放在了英国掌握海上主导权的关键因素上，认为英国的全球影响力及其经济繁荣并非源自其强大的海军实力。事实上，二者之间恰恰是一种反向的因果关系。[1]英国强大的经济实力才是其海上霸主地位的真正保障。

肯尼迪于1980年出版了另一部重要著作——《英德对抗之缘起：1860—1914》。与其他作品一样，作者在该书中也谈及了不同层面的政治生活中的对抗，尤其是国际外交和国内政治。作者同样提出了"（造成英德关系紧张的）深层原因……是经济因素"这样的理论。[2]19世纪德国的政治统一与经济发展都表明，德意志民族有走向社会主义*（工业和资源均掌握在人民手中的一种政治制度）的趋向，当不同地区的人民呼吁国内政治要民主化时，这一趋势更加明显。处于执政地位的德意志精英们采取了所谓的"世界政策"*来应对，意在唤起民众强烈的民族自豪感，希望能通过不断加强军事实力的方法最终把德意志变成像邻国法、俄那样的强国。**世界政策**（Weltpolitik）实质上就是一种强硬的外交政策，即重新崛起的德意志要与欧洲邻国平起平坐，要用强大的海军和强势的外交把自己打造成一个强大的帝国。

> "虽说该书刚出版时的影响不好评说，但随着时间的推移，该书却产生了积极影响，很快便成为了国际畅销书，被译成了 23 种语言。去年，中国还发行了一部以该书为基础的 10 集电视纪录片，并配有重印本。"
>
> —— 约翰·克雷斯："保罗·肯尼迪：新保守派的梦魇"，《卫报》

整合

肯尼迪早期成果的研究话题相对固定。1987 年《大国的兴衰》出版之时，已有学者写了大量的文章，探讨经济繁荣（或衰退）与政治命运之间的关系。《大国的兴衰》出版之后，肯尼迪不断拓宽着自己的研究话题和研究目的。

在 1993 年出版的《为 21 世纪做准备》一书中，肯尼迪的主要分析对象已从"民族国家"变为了跨国组织。他认为，人口增长、资源短缺、环境恶化以及全球范围内不断扩大的贫富差距将从根本上淡化民族国家的概念。在他看来，民族国家就是欧洲的一个机构而已，并且过于孤立而无法处理全球性问题。[3] 他认为，解决相互关联的全球性问题的唯一方法就是提高领导层的国际化水平。

在 2006 年出版的《人类议会》一书中，肯尼迪延续了他在

《为 21 世纪做准备》中所透露出的悲观情绪。不过，这一次他心中已有解决问题的方案，即依靠联合国这个全球性机构去促进各国之间的合作。诚然，联合国也有自身的问题。它还不能制定权威性的规则，在很大程度上仍然考虑的是尊重民族国家的主权。但从理论上讲，联合国还是为人类提供了协调全球力量的最佳机会，这样就可以尝试着去解决那些单凭一国之力无法解决的跨国性问题。研究国际关系的美国学者约翰·伊肯伯里*写道，肯尼迪在《人类议会》中着重讲述了联合国是如何在"支持社会和政治进步"以及"维护和平和促进人权"方面取得一些成绩的。如果我们能将这些胜利再继续下去，人类就还有为生存而奋斗的机会。[4]

肯尼迪以前的研究对象"大国"在这些最新的研究中都扮演着某种特定的角色。但是，一个根本性的问题是它们"合作……的能力极不稳定且稍纵即逝"。[5]

意义

显然，《大国的兴衰》没有预测到苏联会很快解体，该书的影响似乎已成为过去。这也许是因为肯尼迪的研究兴趣转向了跨国问题，然而，他这一早期作品仍有其意义。虽然肯尼迪只是将《大国的兴衰》中最后讨论美国衰落可能性的那几章视为前面主要章节的补充，但人们认为，正是这一部分的内容才更具价值。

尽管英国记者约翰·克雷斯*曾写道，"肯尼迪的新书《大国的兴衰》触到了世界的痛处"，但这并非肯尼迪的本意。他本人在接受采访时说："那本书其实就是对过去五百多年世界上一些大帝国进行的历史研究……但我认为不会有太多人去阅读后面关于美国和苏联的章节。"[6]

英国著名的财经期刊《经济学人》*指出，肯尼迪的观点"看上去不太成熟"，[7] 因为他的著作是在冷战结束前出版的。但在千年之交，随着美国在伊拉克*和阿富汗*不断投入兵力，几年之后又受全球金融危机所困，"这样的情景开始有点像肯尼迪教授所判断的样子了"。[8]

最终，肯尼迪的书成了美国人焦虑的象征，他们担心自己的国家会像以前的大国一样走向衰落。肯尼迪在这个问题上仍然有很强的影响力。他的书出版已有几十年了，但美国的政策制定者仍把他视为美国衰落论的权威顾问。

---

1. 保罗·肯尼迪：《英国海上霸权的兴衰》，伦敦：艾伦莱恩出版公司，1976 年，第 140 页。

2. 保罗·肯尼迪：《英德对抗之缘起：1860—1914》，伦敦：乔治艾伦与恩文出版公司，1980 年，第 464 页。

3. 尼尔·阿彻森："保罗·肯尼迪访谈"，《独立报》，1993 年 3 月 28 日，登录日期 2015 年 9 月 12 日，http://www.independent.co.uk/voices/interview-prepare-to-meet-thy-future-big-books-about-the-21st-century-are-supposed-to-make-your-flesh-creep-but-paul-kennedy-argues-that-the-end-of-the-world-is-not-quite-nigh-1500508.html。

4. 约翰·伊肯伯里："书评：《人类议会》"，《外交事务》第 85 卷，2006 年第 6 期，第 156 页。

5. 伊肯伯里："书评"，第 156 页。

6. 约翰·克雷斯："保罗·肯尼迪：新保守派的梦魇"，《卫报》，2008 年 2 月 5 日，登录日期 2015 年 9 月 3 日，http://www.theguardian.com/education/2008/feb/05/academicexperts.highereducationprofile。

7. 约翰·伊肯伯里："帝国过度扩张？"，《经济学人》，2002 年 6 月 27 日，登录日期 2015 年 9 月 12 日，http://www.economist.com/node/1188741。

8. 伊肯伯里："帝国过度扩张？"。

第三部分：学术影响

9 最初反响

要点 ⚷

- 批评者认为，肯尼迪的理论过于宽泛，许多假设都没有考虑国内优先发展事项和外交策略等因素的作用。

- 肯尼迪回应说，批评者将他的理论过于简单化了，而且他们太过于关注短期效应了。

- 《大国的兴衰》出版四年后，冷战结束。此后，评论家分为了两大阵营：认为美国会成为唯一超级大国的论者和认为世界的分极 * 会由单极向多极转化的论者。

批评

保罗·肯尼迪的《大国的兴衰》很快便成了学界议论的焦点，人们对该书褒贬不一。美国军事战略家爱德华·卢特瓦克 * 评述道，肯尼迪不像是以"历史学家"的身份在写书，他更像是一位有理论思想的"政论家"。[1] 卢特瓦克说，肯尼迪并没有拿自己的理论与其他人的理论进行对比，但肯尼迪断言，不同社会有着不同的发展速度，因为"事实如此"。卢特瓦克指出："比如说，他并不认为不同社会之所以会有不同的发展速度是因为它们的优先发展战略不同。"[2]

美国政治战略家小约瑟夫·奈 * 则认为，我们需要对权力概念进行重构，在后冷战时代尤其如此。奈创造了"软实力"这样的术语，用以表示"通常与军事和经济实力等有形资源相关的硬实力"之外的东西。"软实力"重在以内涵而非外力服众。[3] 软实力包括技术、大众文化和在国际机构中的领导地位。当全世界都在听美国流行音乐时，美国人便可合理获取经济回报，并扩大美国文化的影响力。风行全球的流行文化如何能增强一个国家的实力？奈称："一个国家如果能在全球流行的交流渠道中占据主导位置，它就有更多的机会宣传自己的文化，进而影响到其他国家的人。"[4]奈的评述说明，肯尼迪的研究可能忽略了我们现在看来与国力相关的一些因素。

还有的批评是针对肯尼迪关于大国权力与经济水平关系的论述。一位美国政治理论家在其标题有趣的书评"谨防历史学家的错误类比"中指出，"减少军事开销并不会自动提高经济增长率"。[5]美国国际事务学教授查尔斯·库普坎*分析了20世纪初大英帝国的衰落情况，以此进一步反驳了肯尼迪的观点。他说，英国当时正在失去经济上的优势，"但这并不是军事开销过度造成的"（相反，英国还在不断缩减其军事开销），而是"因为其他国家的经济在快速增长，而英国的工业还未适应新的技术变革"。[6]20世纪，新兴工业国韩国*在有地区竞争对手的情况下，不仅"享有很高的经济增长率，同时还保持着相对较高的军费开销"。[7]库普坎认为，军事支出虽然多数时候会对经济有害，但有时也会带来好处，例如，在军事研究过程中经常会有新的技术诞生。他总结说，肯尼迪提出的因果关系定义不清，那或许只是多种可能关系中的一种。

> "肯尼迪的预测在过去的十多年里并未得到较好印证。俄罗斯的实力确实还在下滑，但其原因并不是肯尼迪认为的那样。俄罗斯在甩掉苏维埃帝国负担并从阿富汗等国撤兵后，仍没有停止下滑的趋势。而肯尼迪预测会走向衰落的其他大国根本就没显出任何衰落的迹象。美国则涅槃重生，不仅在冷战中'获胜'，而且再一次登上了世界经济霸主的宝座。"
>
> ——亨利·诺："为什么《大国的兴衰》搞错了"

回应

肯尼迪认为，卢特瓦克过度简化了他的理论。诚然，大国过度扩张会力不从心，最终会轰然倒下。但这在解释不同国家为何会有不同国力及影响力的问题上只是"附带原因，而非主要原因"。[8] 肯尼迪在解释自己的观点时，稍微做了一些变通。从大国的情况（包括美国在内）来看，"**从长期来看，一个国家的生产力水平与其财政收入水平以及军事实力之间有显著的相关性**"。[9]

肯尼迪认为大国的经济衰退与军事衰落之间存在一个滞后期，这对理解过度扩张概念来说非常重要。当一个国家面临衰落时，其战略投入自然会超出其经济能力。这就加速了其衰落的进程。[10] 从本质上讲，二者是互相影响的：经济衰退先于过度扩张，而过度扩张会使经济难以复苏。冷战后期，即便美国大幅缩减了其军费开支，但其支出在美国当时的经济情况下仍显得相对较高，这就是一个很大的问题。当然，库普坎同样可以用这一点来反驳肯尼迪。

库普坎批评肯尼迪的理论过于概括，还批评他把经济和军事之间的关系想得过于简单。肯尼迪则辩称，帝国过度扩张和经济衰退往往是结伴而行的，他并没有说军事开销就会直接导致经济衰退。

冲突与共识

《大国的兴衰》出版仅四年后，冷战即宣告结束。人们普遍认为世界进入了"单极化"时代，即美国成了世界上唯一的超级大国。这一观点是由美国政治评论家查尔斯·克劳萨默*首先提出的。他坚称："后冷战时期的世界格局不是多极化……美国这一超级大国无可争辩地成了世界的权力中心，并得到了西方盟友的拥护。"[11] 实际上在克劳萨默等人看来，不断扩张的美国根本就没有衰落，仍然是一个超级大国，而且是**唯一的**超级大国，任何国家都无法撼动其地位。关于美国的未来，大致有两种观点：美国终会走向衰落；美国还将保持其唯一超级大国的地位。

肯尼迪预测，冷战结束后美国会走向衰落；美国政治学家亨利·诺*对此预测进行了批判。诺在"为什么《大国的兴衰》搞错了"一文中措辞严厉地指出，肯尼迪忽略了国家身份及国内政治对整个局势的影响。他认为，历史不只是大国兴衰的故事。在他看来，"民主国家最容易创造财富和提升自身实力"，这样，无需借助过多的军事手段，这些国家就能保持相对和平的环境和较高的生产力水平。[12] 诺认为，美国之所以不会像历史上的大国那样容易走向衰落，本质上得益于其尊重选举权利和私人财富的、民主的资本主义社会制度。美国的政治和经济体制完全可以打破肯尼迪所发现的衰落规律。肯尼迪并未直接反驳诺的观点，而是暗示说，"十几年后，再对他的预测进行评价可能会更合适些"——这也就是 2010 年左右。[13]

---

1. 保罗·肯尼迪和爱德华·卢特瓦克："大国兴衰：思想交流"，《美国学者》第 59 卷，1990 年第 2 期，第 287 页。

2. 肯尼迪和卢特瓦克："大国兴衰"，第 289 页。

3. 小约瑟夫·奈："世界权力的变化本质"，《政治科学季刊》第 105 卷，1990 年第 2 期，第 181 页。

4. 小约瑟夫·奈："软实力"，《外交政策》，1990 年第 80 期，第 169 页。

5. W. W. 罗斯托:"谨防历史学家的错误类比",《外交事务》第 66 卷,1998 年第 4 期,第 868 页。

6. 查尔斯·库普坎:"帝国、军事大国和经济衰退",《国际安全》第 13 卷,1989 年第 4 期,第 42 页。

7. 库普坎:"帝国、军事大国和经济衰退",第 45 页。

8. 肯尼迪和卢特瓦克:"大国兴衰",第 285 页。

9. 肯尼迪和卢特瓦克:"大国兴衰",第 285 页。

10. 肯尼迪和卢特瓦克:"大国兴衰",第 285 页。

11. 查尔斯·克劳萨默:"单极时刻",《外交关系》第 70 卷,1990/1991 年第 1 期,第 23 页。

12. 亨利·诺:"为什么《大国的兴衰》搞错了",《国际研究评论》第 27 卷,2001 年第 4 期,第 592 页。

13. 诺:"为什么《大国的兴衰》搞错了",第 580 页。

10 后续争议

要点 🔑

- 人们对美国衰落问题的讨论一直在继续，即使在 2001 年 9 月 11 日恐怖袭击事件（9·11 事件）发生以及"反恐战争"*（美国在中东和非洲发动反恐怖组织的军事行动）中出现诸多问题后，讨论也未停止过。

- "大历史"*这一术语是指在较长时期内对一个主要概念或一种类别（的事件）进行分析的历史研究。

- 印度裔美国作家法里德·扎卡利亚*可能是当今美国衰落问题研究领域里最重要的人物；他认为，在整个世界向"后美国"转变之时，如果美国能对其他民族多一些宽容，或许可保住自己的威望。

应用与问题

保罗·肯尼迪于 1987 年出版《大国的兴衰》后，美国似乎在 20 世纪 90 年代都拥有无可撼动的超级大国地位。因此，在 21 世纪初，人们已很少再提及肯尼迪的"衰落论"了。2002 年，肯尼迪的观点发生了重大改变，他在《金融时报》*上发文称，美国保持了其单极世界的霸主*——即统治地位。然而，他紧跟着又谨慎地分析说，美国能保住这一地位"主要得益于其过去十年间令人瞩目的经济增长"。但自 2001 年 9 月 11 日遭到恐怖袭击后，美国便加大了军事投入。在这样的背景下，经济增长一旦停止，美国便会再度陷入"过度投入风险"之中。[1]

2003 年，肯尼迪、美国政治战略家小约瑟夫·奈和政治顾问理查德·珀尔*都参加了"'不情愿的帝国'学术研讨会",他们所在的小组主要讨论的是美国在后9·11时代,特别是考虑到伊拉克战争,应该如何保证自身的安全。肯尼迪概括了他关于经济的观点,认为美国在伊拉克的持久战会影响到其国内的繁荣。但大部分时间里,他都在谈论战争对美国"软实力"*的影响。他说,战争不仅夺去了众多平民的生命,还降低了国际组织的权威性,因为美国未经联合国授权就单方面发动了战争。[2]

肯尼迪对伊拉克战争给美国"软实力"造成影响的讨论表明,他的评论不只局限在经济与战略的关系上。肯尼迪认为美国最终是想在安全投入上营造一种"帝国"模式,因为美国虽然拥有"全球影响力,但这一身份与其人口不到世界人口的百分之五这一事实不相匹配"。[3]

9·11事件后,美国重启了在海外的准帝国承诺,而2007—2008年的金融危机*又使其国内的经济雪上加霜。在此背景下,肯尼迪再次提出了美国衰落论。他在美国财经报纸《华尔街日报》*上发表文章说:"截至目前的数据表明,中国和印度的经济正在增长(虽不及过去快,但仍在增长),而美国的经济则明显处于萎缩期。"因此,美国在全球生产总量中所占的份额不可能保持前些年那样的水平。[4]他总结道,这种情况预示着"全球构造力中心正在发生转移",由美国转向了太平洋西边的亚洲。美国政府应该为发生这样的转移承担责任。

> "新世纪最重要的政治现象就是亚洲的相对崛起,尤其是中国的崛起,与此相对的则是整个西方的相对衰落,尤其是欧洲和美国这两大经济体的相对衰落。"
>
> ——保罗·肯尼迪:《大国的兴衰》

思想流派

《大国的兴衰》可被看作一部与历史学和政治学都相关的学术专著。肯尼迪自己则将其视为关于"大历史"研究的专著，即"作者在一册书中围绕一个宏观问题进行研究，彻底理解透彻后，再将其理解的内容讲述给读者"。[5]"大历史"实际上就是研究历史的一种理论方法，旨在对大类别事件做出解释。肯尼迪在写《大国的兴衰》时，大类别事件就是指大国的相对实力。同一研究领域的学者苏格兰历史学家尼尔·弗格森*的著作也广受欢迎，但他关注的大类别事件是西方对全球的主导地位及其他国家对西方主导地位的威胁。弗格森指出，若有人在 1500 年就认为西欧将会主导整个世界，那他"简直就是在异想天开"。但他又问道："那 15 世纪后的西欧文明又是凭什么超越了物质富裕的东方帝国呢？"[6]弗格森对西方的优势进行了探究，这样"我们才可能评判……我们当下的兴衰问题了"。[7]

当前研究

法里德·扎卡里亚也许是当今世界上最具影响力的"衰退论者"（持"美国的实力和影响力正在衰落"观点的人）。他于 2009 年出版了专著《后美国世界》后名声鹊起。扎卡里亚指出，"1989 年以来的大约二十年时间里，美国凭借自身实力逐渐决定了国际秩序"，这意味着美国成了全球唯一相关的政治参与者。这种状况是一系列包括经济和军事等复杂因素共同作用的结果，冷战之后的美国成了唯一的超级大国。

但今天的世界政治已在发生变化。[8]即便世界秩序继续由逐渐衰微的美国来决定，美国也需将诸如中国、俄罗斯、欧盟*等"其他几支重要力量"的意见考虑在内，即形成扎卡里亚所谓的"综合各方意见后的决断力和能动性"。[9]但扎卡里亚同时也指出，虽然美国的经济和军事实力与处于上升期的国家对比时表现出了相对衰落的态势，但目前还没有其他的国家试图要取代美国的位置。事实的真相是，这些新崛起的力量只不过是更关注相互提防。扎卡里亚认为美国的强大之处在于其社会的开放性，他建议为了避免世界不断向"后美国化"方向发展，美国就需不断提高其社会开放度和包容度。[10]在扎卡里亚看来，开放的心态会鼓励他人行善，让国民发挥出最大的潜能，还能从海外吸引来优秀人才。

1. 保罗·肯尼迪："雄鹰已着陆"，《金融时报》，2002年2月1日。

2. 保罗·肯尼迪等："不情愿的帝国：结果重大的时代"，《布朗世界事务》第10卷，2003年第1期，第16页。

3. 肯尼迪等："不情愿的帝国"，第16页。

4. 保罗·肯尼迪："美国实力在衰退"，《华尔街日报》，2009年1月1日，登录日期2015年9月14日，http://www.wsj.com/articles/SB123189377673479433。

5. 保罗·肯尼迪："遥远的地平线：关于美国的未来'大历史'会告诉我们什么？"，《外交事务》第87卷，2008年第3期，第126—127页。

6. 尼尔·弗格森：《文明：西方和其他世界》，伦敦：艾伦莱恩出版社，2010年，第8页。

7. 弗格森：《文明》，第18页。

8. 法里德·扎卡里亚：《后美国世界》，纽约：W. W. 诺顿出版公司，2008年，第42页。

9. 扎卡里亚：《后美国世界》，第43页。

10. 扎卡里亚：《后美国世界》，第257页。

11 当代印迹

要点 ✑━━

- 《大国的兴衰》为当代人所知，是因为它提到了美国的衰落以及美国该如何应对其霸权地位受到中国挑战等重要问题。

- 有观点认为，美国应该克服自身实力衰退的影响，勇于承担全球领导者的责任；这样，美国就能够用相对较少的付出获得（在议程安排、软实力提升和经济收益等方面）较为丰厚的回报。

- 反对者认为，参与全球性事务未必就是利大于弊。他们建议美国重新考虑其在国际事务中所扮演的角色，以便能持续发挥作用。

地位

保罗·肯尼迪是将《大国的兴衰》作为一部历史学著作进行创作的，其历史跨度上至 1500 年，下至 20 世纪下半叶。但在关注国家衰落的美国人眼里，该书更像是一本政治学专著。当今许多研究国际关系的学者将兴趣放在了霸权问题上而非单纯的国力问题，所以在他们的研究中，肯尼迪对国际体系的分析方法似乎不大适用。

意大利政治经济学家乔万尼·阿里吉*通过对"世界霸权"概念的讨论，为我们提供了理解欧洲"大国"竞争概念的另一种视角。他认为，世界霸权就是"一个国家行使领导和统治其他主权国家体系的权力"。[1] 因为"霸权"实质上就是规定和统治国际体系的能力，所以"霸权"概念要比"大国"概念更能引起像阿里吉这样的国际历史理论家们的研究兴趣。他们发现将大国视为欧洲的独有现象是毫无意义的。在他们看来，欧洲人正对世界其他各地实施着霸权统治，并按自己的想象定义整个世界体系。

在建议美国应该如何行事这一方面，《大国的兴衰》并未起到决定性的作用。但该书提出了美国正处于衰落期这一观点，指出"美国的结构性矛盾以及财政和经济问题会随着时间的推移渐渐使美国失去其作为大国的基础"。[2]但20世纪90年代，美国迎来了前所未有的发展，享有很高的国际威望。于是，一些学者便放弃了衰退论思想。但据美国学者克里斯托夫·莱恩*的调查，2007—2008年金融危机过后，衰退论又引起了学者们的重视。[3]旨在影响美国对外政策的有影响力的智囊团布鲁金斯学会*发布了一项标志性的研究报告，认为中国的崛起是造成美国"相对衰落"的根源。中国的地区影响力日益增强，这在很大程度上得益于其飞速增长的经济实力。经济实力的增长又使其军事实力不断增强。[4]布鲁金斯学会的报告将中美关系定义成了一种"战略互不信任"关系，即双方都"认为对方会为了实现其主要的长期目标而损害己方的核心利益和前途"。[5]

> "现代史上曾出现过两种国际秩序：**英式和平和美式和平**。英美两国在各自强权统治时期都建起了各自主导的国际格局，为各自的经济利益和地缘政治目的服务。不过，两国也给作为整体的国际体系带来了重要利益——公共产品。"
>
> —— 克里斯托夫·莱恩："美式和平的终结"

互动

肯尼迪认为，处于全球领导地位的国家在衰退期会陷入两难的境地——经济实力在下降，海外战略投入需增加。面对如此困境，要想保住原来的威望，是应该加大还是减少军事投入呢？[6]美国学者斯蒂芬·布鲁克斯 *、约翰·伊肯伯里和威廉·沃尔福斯 * 在 2013 年发表的一篇文章"负重前行"中写道："华盛顿可能想……从世界事务中抽身出来。崛起的中国正在削弱美国的领导地位，（而）美国的财政预算危机则要求美国减少国防开支。"[7] 考虑到这种形势，三位作者支持美国加大国际投入的做法；他们解释说，美国可以缩减战略投入，在军事和经济投入之间找到平衡点，这样就可以避免"帝国过度扩张"。美国加大全球性投入虽然会付出较高的代价，但这样做对国家繁荣的贡献却远超我们想象。用作者的话说："军事上的优势可以巩固其在经济上的领导地位。"[8]

美国的全球统治地位能使其以多种重要方式享有公共利益。美国海军能确保海上航道的安全。美元是世界通用的储备货币 *。美国可以通过经济杠杆支持盟友进行军事投入。美国可以通过双边协定方式或在北约 * 框架下为盟友提供安全保障，为其节省大笔国防预算。[9] 美国的投入虽然巨大，但却从中收获了超高的回报。正因为有美国的帮助，"世界上最重要的地区才没有爆发冲突，全球经济才能依然活跃，国际合作才变得更为顺畅"。美国也因此可以塑造世界的面貌。[10]

持续争议

美国政治学家巴里·波森 * 的一篇文章"战略撤退"可以视为"负重前行"的姊妹篇。波森认同肯尼迪的观点，即美国应该尽量少卷入全球性事务之中。肯尼迪在《大国的兴衰》中写道："在未来的几十年里，美国政治家要认识到全球发展的大趋势，有必要合理'应对'各项事务，好让美国地位下降的过程变得相对缓慢平稳一些。"[11]

波森认为，美国应该慢慢减少世界对其依赖的程度，从容应对自身的衰落。比如说，美国承担了许多欧亚盟国的国防重担，为了推进自己制定的国际议程，美国还卷入了许多海外冲突，这些都带来了如下严重的后果："敌人永远也消灭不完；盟国不愿为自己的国防投入；大国抱团反对华盛顿的计划，进一步提高了外交政策的执行成本。"[12]

波森认为美国是在单凭自己的力量维护着全球的安全。美国长期承担着某些战败国的防务任务，并与中国台湾、日本和欧洲签有长期安全防务协议，但其他国家和地区并未承担维护全球安全的责任。在需要打击恐怖主义的那些国家里，波森主张采取一种"灵活"的总体战略，"慎用武力，不必像在阿富汗那样付出重建家园般的努力"。[13]从根本上讲，"如果美国的债务不断增长，且权力继续向其他国家分化，未来就可能会出现某种经济或政治危机，迫使华盛顿突然改变其战略路线"。[14]如果美国迅速撤退的话，就会出现权力真空地带，诸如中国等其他大国就会扮演起领导者的角色。

---

1. 乔万尼·阿里吉：《漫长的 20 世纪：金钱、权力和我们时代的起源》，伦敦：沃索出版社，2002 年，第 27 页。

2. 克里斯托夫·莱恩："美式和平的终结：西方衰落缘何不可避免"，《大西洋月刊》，2012 年 4 月，登录时间 2015 年 9 月 14 日，http://www.theatlantic.com/international/archive/2012/04/the-end-of-pax-americana-how-western-decline-became-inevitable/256388/。

3. 莱恩："美式和平的终结"。

4. 李侃如和王辑思：《中美战略互疑》，华盛顿特区：布鲁金斯学会，2012年，第2—3页。

5. 李侃如和王辑思：《中美战略互疑》，第5页。

6. 保罗·肯尼迪：《大国的兴衰》，纽约：温特吉出版社，1989年，第533页。

7. 斯蒂芬·布鲁克斯等："负重前行：支持美国履行国际义务"，《外交事务》第92卷，2013年第1期，第130页。

8. 布鲁克斯等："负重前行"，第138页。

9. 布鲁克斯等："负重前行"，第138页。

10. 布鲁克斯等："负重前行"，第139页。

11. 肯尼迪：《大国的兴衰》，第534页。

12. 巴里·波森："战略撤退：实施非积极外交政策的情况"，《外交事务》第92卷，2013年第1期，第117页。

13. 波森："战略撤退"，第122页。

14. 波森："战略撤退"，第128页。

12 未来展望

要点 🔑

- 肯尼迪最近发文称，与美国相比，中国在经济和军事方面正处于上升趋势。

- 美国律师、学者菲利普·博比特 * 认为 21 世纪的战争形态已发生变化。过去，只有国家参与才可能引发大规模的动乱。今天，技术让那些资金不足的小型组织也能成为暴乱制造者。

- 《大国的兴衰》虽然是一部重要的历史著作，但因为该书对冷战后的美国做出了走向衰落的预测，所以还引发了政治学研究领域的关注和讨论。

潜力

　　虽然《大国的兴衰》是国际史研究方面的一部重要著作，但其作者保罗·肯尼迪因为在该书最后章节里论及了美国会走向衰落的问题，所以他也一直在积极参与美国应该如何应对衰落这一问题的讨论。肯尼迪指出，"亚洲的发展速度明显快于美国和欧洲这样的成熟经济体"，特别是在资本平衡配置方面。[1] 他指出："一个国家出现银行存款结余通常意味着其军事—政治平衡将会发生改变——从伦巴第大区到安特卫普和阿姆斯特丹；再从那里到伦敦；从伦敦——到纽约；再从纽约——到哪里？上海？"简言之，亚洲已经变得越来越富裕了，从经济角度考虑，其重要性已超过了西方。

　　军事平衡方面也发生了变化，海上实力（包括航空母舰）的变化尤为明显。肯尼迪认为美国战略家一定会问："中国为什么会在国防上投入那么多钱？"虽然中国的国防预算从绝对数字看仍然较低，但是否一直在增长呢？"他们为什么要投巨资研发网络战争、军事卫星和商业侦察呢？还有在美国战舰雷达屏幕下方飞行的中程掠海导弹以及跨越太平洋的超远程火箭应该怎么解释呢？"[2] 如果中国的海军实力正处于**相对的**上升期（因而会扩大其在世界范围的影响），那么美国对太平洋的控制权不是就受到影响了吗？要知道，拥有太平洋就等于拥有了半个世界。在《大国的兴衰》中，肯尼迪认为大国的实力可以从财政实力和军事实力两方面去衡量。因此，中国的实力似乎在不断增长，而美国的实力则在不断减弱；两相比较，我们可能正在目睹一个大国走向衰落的过程。

> "我们必须为反恐行动中的国家行为尽快制定法律和战略上的依据。这实质上就是从有关主权的法律概念出发，赋予反恐行为以正当理由，承认这是合法合理的治理行为。"
>
> —— 菲利普·博比特：《恐怖与认同》

未来方向

菲利普·博比特是继肯尼迪之后关注美国世界地位的又一位著名学者。他在自己的两部著作《阿喀琉斯之盾：战争、和平与历史进程》（2002）和《恐怖与认同：21 世纪的战争》（2008）中为读者描绘了处于技术变革、宪制变革和经济变革时代的全球历史画面。他指出，美国在中东和非洲发动大范围"反恐战争的目的不是要征服领土，也不是要压制某种意识形态"，即不是保罗·肯尼迪所认为的那种战争。相反，博比特认为反恐战争能"确保认同型国家享有安全的环境，让敌人无法强迫或诱使恐怖型国家采取行动"。[3]

博比特所谓的"认同型国家"是指那些获得公民认同而合法存在的西方国家，这些国家的首要任务是保护其民众的安全。但国家保护在技术不断发展与全球互通的今天面临着许多新的挑战。比如，威胁国家的敌人在哪里？博比特对处于新时期敌人威胁之下的美国的实力做了评价，该评价与肯尼迪在《大国的兴衰》中的评价形成了鲜明的对比。博比特称，美国是世界上最大的经济体，拥有"一支武器和通信装备超级精良的庞大军队"。但"美国因此遭到的潜在危害（因为技术在扩散的过程中会变得越来越廉价）却要比技术带来的安全感上升得还要快"。[4]

换言之，博比特认为技术已经改变了肯尼迪于20世纪末分析得出的战争动因。曾经，只有国家才有实力发动大规模的战争，而实力又是由强大的经济所决定的。发动这样的战争需要有多方面的资源保障，只有国家可以承担得起。博比特认为，在和恐怖主义作斗争的今天，与军事和经济实力相比，国家之间的凝聚力和战略上的精诚合作显得更为重要。如果各国能够紧密联系，就能准确预测威胁，从而免遭灾难。

小结

保罗·肯尼迪的《大国的兴衰》首先是一部历史专著。在该书中，肯尼迪对1500年以来世界上主要的大国进行了分析研究，总结了这些大国之所以能成为大国的原因。他同时也指出了一些可能会导致大国失去其地位的因素。尽管该书对历史有着深入透彻的分析，但更多的学者还是将其视为了政治学专著。该书的最后几章是作者在主体内容完成后又附加上去的内容，该部分内容结合时局，阐述了美国会走向衰落的思想。

　　肯尼迪认为，国家战略和经济水平紧密相连。一个国家如果经济持续增长，生产能力超级强大，那么其国家地位自然就会显著提升。工农业产值是经济繁荣的基础，肯尼迪衡量了工农业的生产力水平，而不是简单地去衡量生产资料。经济繁荣的国家必定拥有强大的军事实力，在任何战场都能无往不胜，"大国"就这样诞生了。但物极必反，当实力增强的国家为了获取更多物质财富而不断投入时，往往就会导致"帝国过度扩张"。于是，这些扩张的大国就像扛着沉重包袱在爬山的老人，而那些经济更具活力、海外投入相对较少的国家就会从大国的投入中获利，最终赶超脚步放缓的前者。

　　肯尼迪的研究不仅是一种（简单但）强大的历史解释范式，而且还兼具向美国发出警报的功能，告诫美国不要在冷战结束时试图去创建自己的"帝国"。否则，美国就会像肯尼迪书中所讲的其他大国那样走上衰落之路。

---

1. 保罗·肯尼迪："亚洲的崛起：崛起与衰落"，《今日世界》第66卷，2010年第8/9期，第7页。
2. 肯尼迪："亚洲的崛起：崛起与衰落"，第7页。
3. 菲利普·博比特：《恐怖与认同：21世纪的战争》，伦敦：企鹅出版社，2009年，第3页。
4. 博比特：《恐怖与认同》，第537页。

术语表

1. **亚伯大学**：英国威尔士的一所研究型大学。

2. **阿富汗战争**：2001 年，以美国为首的北约对基地组织和塔利班发动的军事打击。

3. **无政府状态**：一种没有行政或管理当局执行规则的状况。

4. **年鉴学派**：一种法国史学研究流派。该流派强调，日常生活模式是长期演化的结果，他们主张用跨学科的方法（采用不同学科的研究方法，这里特指地理学、经济学和社会学的研究方法）进行时间跨度较长的历史研究。这种方法与传统的历史研究不同，传统的研究方法是将重大事件以时间发展顺序进行呈现的。

5. **外交政策（Außenpolitik）**：意思为"外部政策"的一个德语术语，认为制定外交政策是一个国家最重要的活动。

6. **大历史**：一种旨在解释较大类别或概念的史学理论研究方法。该术语近来也用于指对从宇宙之初到当下时代整个时间段内所发生历史的研究。

7. **两极化**：相互对立的两个大国主导下的国际秩序。

8. **大英帝国（16 至 20 世纪）**：指世界上由英国直接统治的所有地区。第一次世界大战后，英国统治的地区占全世界土地面积的 25%，地区人口占全世界人口的 20%。虽然大英帝国在二战后出现了严重的衰退，但学者们普遍认为 1997 年香港回归中国才是其终结的标志。

9. **布鲁金斯学会**：世界上最具影响力的美国智囊团，为美国制定合理外交政策出谋划策。总体而言，该智囊团支持更加开放和互联的国际体系。

10. **资本主义**：强调私有产权、私有产业以追求利润为目标的经济制度。

11. **冷战（1947—1991）**：美国和苏联关系紧张的历史时期。在该时期，两国虽然从未直接交手，但都卷入了一系列秘密战争、代理战争和间谍战。

12. **共产主义**：主张生产资料国有化、劳动集体化和社会阶层平等化的政治意识形态。这曾是苏联（1917—1989）的意识形态，与冷战时期以自由市场为特征的资本主义形成了鲜明对比。

13. **古巴导弹危机（1962）**：最有可能引发美苏两国爆发核战的一次危机，由苏联在古巴部署战略导弹事件而引起。

14. **衰落主义 / 论**：认为自己的国家或机构在世界上所处的整体地位正处于不可逆转的下行期。

15. **王朝**：元首均来自一个家族的国家团体。

16. **《经济学人》**：1843 年于伦敦创办的一份英文杂志，以刊登较为深入分析经济和政治问题的文章为其主要特色。杂志主编倾向"古典自由主义"的立场，倡导自由企业机制和个人自由精神。

17. **欧洲联盟**：1993 年成立的跨国和跨政府组织，简称欧盟。欧盟负责管理和协调 28 个欧洲国家的利益，制定统一的政策。

18. **马岛战争（1982）**：阿根廷和英国为争夺位于南大西洋的福克兰群岛而爆发的战争。战争造成将近 1 000 人丧生，以英国获胜告终。

19. **金融危机（2007—2008）**：20 世纪 30 年代以来最严重的一次经济萧条期。这段时间内，全球范围内的失业率在上升，经济产值在下降。

20. **《金融时报》**：1888 年在伦敦创办的一家英文报纸，主要刊登商业和经济相关内容的文章。

21. **《外交事务》**：由位于纽约的美国外交关系委员会于 1921 年创办的一份专业性学术期刊，主要发表国际政治研究方面的文章。

22. **国民生产总值（GNP）**：一个国家的居民在一年内生产的所有产品和提供的所有服务的市场价值总和。

23. **哈布斯堡王朝**（1438—1918）：欧洲历史上统治领域最广的王室家族，其鼎盛时期曾统治着意大利南部、西班牙、奥地利、德意志城邦国、匈牙利以及中欧和西欧的其他地区。哈布斯堡王朝习惯通过联姻的方式而非武力征服的手段来加强其政治影响力。

24. **霸权**：一个关于单一个体统治整个群体的概念，"霸主"不仅有权决定他人做或不做什么，而且实际上还在按自己的意愿建立"游戏规则"。

25. **兴登堡计划**（1916）：第一次世界大战中，德国为了大幅提高军工产品产量而采取的政策。该计划（即整个德国经济以"战争相关"的产业为导向）最终导致了灾难和饥荒，德国随后也走向了衰落。

26. **神圣罗马帝国**：从9世纪起一直持续到1806年横跨西欧和中欧的封建君主制帝国，其疆域包括了奥地利大部、尼德兰、那不勒斯以及欧洲周边的其他领土。

27. **国际关系**：对全球体系下国家之间关系的研究，主要研究各国的外交政策。此外，世界银行及其他非政府组织（NGOs）等跨国组织也是其研究的对象。

28. **伊拉克战争**（2003—2011）：最初为伊拉克和美国之间爆发的武装冲突，后来演变为一场持久的反抗与镇压的拉锯战。美国及其盟友认为当时的伊拉克领导人萨达姆·侯赛因秘密储备了大量的核武器。

29. **朝鲜战争**（1950—1953）：二战结束后，冷战局势紧张，南北朝鲜分裂，最终二者之间爆发了战争。以美国为首的联合国部队支持南朝鲜；中国在苏联的帮助下支持北朝鲜。

30. **长时段**（Longue durée）：意为"长期"的一个法语术语。在历史学语境下，该术语指的是法国年鉴学派的历史研究方法，即观察较长时间跨度内的历史变化（往往也是社会变化）。

31. **明王朝**（1368—1644）：中国历史上的一个朝代。明朝统治者加强中央集权，设有自己的常备军队。明王朝还因修建长城之类气势恢宏的工程而闻名于世。

32. **蒙古帝国**（1206—1368）：指蒙古军阀铁木真（即成吉思汗）与其后代征服亚欧大陆后所统治的整个疆域，鼎盛时期的蒙古帝国包括从东南亚到东欧127万平方英里的辽阔疆域。

33. **多极化**：多个大国具有同等重要地位的国际秩序。

34. **北约**（NATO）：即北大西洋公约组织，是一个政府间的军事同盟，同盟中的成员在遭到外来攻击时，会得到其他成员的集体保护。该组织由美国领导，共有28个成员国，包括了所有的欧洲主要国家。该组织由美、英、法、加等国于1949年二战结束后签署的《北大西洋公约》演化而来。

35. **纽卡斯尔大学**：1963年成立于纽卡斯尔的一所公立研究型大学。

36. **9·11事件**：指2001年9月11日，伊斯兰极端组织——基地组织向美国协同发动的四起恐怖袭击事件。四架民用客机被恐怖分子劫持后当作了攻击美国国内某些建筑的工具，这些建筑包括：纽约世贸中心的双子塔和华盛顿特区的五角大楼。

37. **范式**：决定某一特定学科理论的世界观。例如，国际关系研究的现实主义范式的核心思想就是：国家之间是相互冲突的，而非合作的。

38. **美式和平**：一个意为"美国式和平"的拉丁语术语，指的是20世纪下半叶全球相对较长的稳定时期（指大国之间，不指一国内部）。但是，大国之间的代理战争却此起彼伏，南半球所有的专制国家也内战不断，这些都让人们对当时的世界和平充满了怀疑。

39. **英式和平**：指19世纪英国的实力处于巅峰状态时，全球处于相对稳定的时期（至少西方大国间关系相对稳定）。

40. **分极**：指国际体系内的权力分布，两极体系的权力集中在两个国家手中，而多极体系的权力集中在多个国家手中。

41. **里根主义**：罗纳德·里根总统任期内执行的一项外交政策，其目的在于削弱苏联的影响力或实力。美国政府对国际反共武装力量进行资助，不惜花费巨额资金为他们提供武器，希望他们能够破坏社会主义国家的稳定。

42. **储备货币**：政府为方便进行国际交易所持有的货币。目前来说，美元是最重要的一种货币，因为本国货币不是美元的两个国家之间进行贸易时是需要用到美元的。

43. **罗马帝国**（公元前27年—公元385年）：以地中海为中心，横跨欧、亚、非的大帝国。朱利叶斯·恺撒自称大帝后，罗马共和国也就变成了罗马帝国。罗马帝国鼎盛时期的疆域不仅包括整个地中海地区，还包括近东的大部分地区。公元385年，帝国分裂为西罗马帝国（北方蛮族入侵后于476年灭亡）和东罗马帝国（即拜占庭帝国，1453年为奥斯曼帝国所灭）。

44. **圣安东尼学院**：牛津大学的一个学院，成立于1950年。该学院只招收研究生，专业为"区域研究"，即对诸如东亚或非洲等特定地理区域的研究。

45. **社会主义**：生产资料（发展工商业所需的工具和资源）公有化的一种社会制度。

46. **软实力**：美国政治思想家小约瑟夫·奈提出的一个概念，实质上就是一种文化帝国主义。美国可凭借在技术和文化方面的优势形成强大的"软实力"，并在这种"软实力"的帮助下，通过联合国这样的国际组织来占据国际管理中的领导地位，而非靠经济或军事因素构成的"硬实力"获取领导地位。

47. **韩国**：位于东亚朝鲜半岛南部的国家，经济高度发达。20世纪60年代以来，韩国与中国香港、新加坡和中国台湾（"亚洲四小龙"）的经济取得了快速的发展。

48. **苏联**（USSR）：一个超国家、横跨欧洲和中亚地区的社会主义国家联盟，首都为莫斯科。苏联于1922年成立，1991年冷战结束后解体。

49. **势力范围**：冷战时期一个非常重要的政治概念。一个国家的"势力范围"包括这个国家在其内可以享有特权的所有地区，甚或其他国家。

50. **超级大国**：常常专指处于冷战时期的美、苏两国，因为这两个国家比历史上任何国家都要强大。

51. **极权（主义）**：一种管理国家的制度，该制度下日常生活中最重要的事情是服从国家的意志和利益。

52. **联合国**：代表了世界上几乎所有国家的国际政府组织，主要负责管理国际卫生、发展、安全及其他类似的事务。

53. **牛津大学**：英国牛津的一所研究型大学，它是英语世界里最古老的一所大学。人们认为，尽管牛津大学最早的学院是13世纪创立的，但牛津的教学活动于11世纪就开始了。牛津大学的不同学院都想争得这份荣誉。

54. **越南战争**：由共产党领导的北越南军和由美国及南越南领导的反共势力之间长达二十年的军事冲突。战争始于1955年，一直持续到美军撤离越南的1975年，这是美国在冷战时期打过的持续时间最长的一场代理战争。

55. **《华尔街日报》**：1889年于纽约创办的一份英文报纸，主要刊登有关商业和经济方面的文章和信息。

56. **反恐战争**：通常指美国在中东地区领导实施的打击包括基地组织在内的非国家恐怖主义者的军事行动，也包括在巴基斯坦实施的无人机行动、占领阿富汗行动，以及其他或隐蔽或公开的军事行动。

57. **《华沙条约》**（1955—1991）：东欧八个社会主义国家为了保证自身安全而成立的军事联盟。冷战结束后，华约组织解散。

58. **世界政策**（Weltpolitik）：一个意为"世界政策"的德语术语，指德意志帝国政府于19世纪末出台的一项政策，该政策实施的目的为：建立一支强大的军队，培养强烈的民族自豪感，利用强硬的外交手段塑造德意志帝国的"大国形象"。

59. **世界体系论**：一种研究历史的整体分析方法，该分析法认为推动历史变革的是把资本、劳动力和其他因素融在一起的"世界体系"，而不是单个的"民族国家"。

60. **第一次世界大战**：发生于1914年至1918年的一场国际战争，欧洲为中心战场，当时世界上的主要经济大国都卷入其中。战争规模的升级和军工技术的进步造成了巨大的军民伤亡。有学者认为第二次世界大战是第一次世界大战的延续，因为一战时期紧张的局势并未得到彻底解决。

61. **第二次世界大战**：1939 年至 1945 年间，席卷全球的一场国际战争，世界上的大国和无数的其他国家都卷入其中。这是一场同盟国（美、英、法、苏等国）与轴心国（德、意、日等国）之间的一场决战，也是一场自由与暴政较量的道义之战。在这场战争中，大屠杀事件曾多次上演。

62. **耶鲁大学**：常春藤联盟大学之一，成立于 1701 年，是美国第三所最早创办的大学。

人名表

1. 乔万尼·阿里吉（1937—2009），意大利政治经济学家、历史学家。他主要研究 1400 年以来国际资本主义的演变及其附带的思想。除了学者的身份外，他还是一名政治活动家，曾于 1966 年在罗得西亚（现津巴布韦）教书时被捕入狱。

2. 奥托·冯·俾斯麦（1815—1898），十九世纪普鲁士政治家。他被认为是现代德国的奠基人，也是德意志帝国的首任总理。

3. 杰里米·布莱克（1955 年生），英国历史学家，是位于英格兰西南部的埃克塞特大学的历史学教授。他是 18 世纪国际关系和英国政治研究方面的专家。

4. 菲利普·博比特（1948 年生），美国律师、公务员、安全研究学者。他在民主党和共和党当政的政府都任过职，主要工作是为美国总统提供情报、国际法和战略方面的建议。

5. 费尔南·布罗代尔（1902—1985），法国历史学家。他是年鉴学派的创始人，强调长期、大范围内的社会经济变化（而非君王决策）在推动历史发展中的作用。

6. 约翰·布鲁尔，加利福尼亚大学洛杉矶分校历史学家，主要研究 17 和 18 世纪的历史。

7. 斯蒂芬·布鲁克斯，达特茅斯大学教授。他是一名支持"前行"政策的公众知识分子。"前行"意味着勇于进行海外投入，在解决全球性问题（经济、军事等方面）中发挥积极的作用。该政策意在提高国家影响力，而非保留资源。

8. 查理五世（1500—1558），西班牙国王（即卡洛斯一世）。他于 1519 年当选为神圣罗马帝国皇帝（中欧地区诸多半独立王国所组成联盟的统治者，由选举产生）。他统治西班牙期间，一方面在新世界不断殖民扩张，一方面在欧洲与法兰西不断争战。

9. 克里斯托弗·哥伦布（1451—1506），意大利探险家。哥伦布本打算去寻找通往印度的海上路线，但却于1492年横渡大西洋后到了美洲。

10. 约翰·克雷斯，英国记者，《卫报》撰稿人。他目前在英国议会下议院从事文书工作。

11. 浮士德博士，德国民间传说中的人物。英国剧作家克里斯托弗·马洛创作的戏剧于1592年首次演出后，浮士德的人物形象便广为人知。据传，浮士德与魔鬼做了一笔交易，用他的灵魂换取了大量知识。

12. 尼尔·弗格森（1964年生），苏格兰历史学家、通俗作家。他的研究兴趣是西方和资本主义在世界史上的特殊作用。他偶尔也会因为对伊斯兰教或殖民主义的评论成为媒体讨伐的对象。

13. 约翰·刘易斯·加迪斯（1941年生），美国耶鲁大学军事及海军史教授。他被认为是冷战研究方面最重要的历史学家，他提倡的"伟人理论"研究方法强调个人在历史进程中的作用。

14. 约翰·安德鲁·加拉格尔（1919—1980），帝国史研究专家，英国牛津和剑桥大学教授。他与他人合著的文章《自由贸易的帝国主义》被称为历史研究领域被引次数最多的文献。

15. 塞缪尔·亨廷顿（1927—2008），美国政治理论家。他于1993年发表的文章《文明的冲突？》（后来写成了一本书）让他声名鹊起。文章认为，在后冷战时代，文化分裂将会引发国际冲突。

16. 约翰·伊肯伯里（1954年生），美国普林斯顿大学国际关系理论家。他是"自由国际主义"美国政策的制定者之一。

17. 查尔斯·克劳萨默（1950—2018），美国公共知识分子、新闻工作者，曾获普利策奖。他主张美国应采取强硬但又克制的外交政策，"里根主义"这一术语是由他首先提出的。

18. 查尔斯·库普坎（1958年生），美国学者、乔治城大学国际事务学教授、外交关系委员会高级研究员。库普坎主要研究国际事务中和平与变化的可能性。

19. 克里斯托夫·莱恩（1949 年生），德克萨斯农业机械大学情报和国家安全研究室主任。他反对自由国际主义者主张向海外传播美国价值观的做法。

20. 理查德·内德·勒博（1942 年生），美国政治学家、伦敦大学国王学院国际政治学教授。他被认为是新古典现实主义的创始人，该学派认为，人格和权力平衡在决定国际结果方面均起着举足轻重的作用。

21. 巴兹尔·利德尔·哈特爵士（1895—1970），英国牛津大学军事理论学家。一战结束后，他建议摒弃静止的、战壕式的作战方式，主张大力发展快速坦克的作战方式。

22. 爱德华·卢特瓦克（1942 年生），美国军事及政治理论家。他的研究方向为"宏观"战略，他曾在著作中描述了早在罗马帝国时期的"宏观"战略。

23. 威廉·麦克尼尔（1917—2016），芝加哥大学加拿大裔美国历史学教授。他在历史学的研究和教学工作中成绩斐然，于 2010 年获得了美国国家人文奖章。

24. 亨利·诺（1941 年生），乔治华盛顿大学政治学和国际事务学教授。里根任美国总统期间，他是美国国家安全委员会的成员。

25. 小约瑟夫·奈（1937 年生），哈佛大学政治学教授。他与美国学者罗伯特·基欧汉的合著《权力与相互依赖》是新自由主义的奠基之作。他也被认为是"复杂相互依赖"理论之父，该理论解释了各国利益相互依赖时，国家之间是如何避免冲突的。

26. 理查德·珀尔（1941 年生），美国政治顾问。他曾任参议院军事委员会议员、里根政府时期国防部助理秘书。目前，除了许多智囊团成员的身份外，他还是一个新保守派组织的重要成员，该组织的成立旨在影响美国的外交政策。

27. 腓力二世（1527—1598）：西班牙国王。他当时还统治着欧洲的其他大片地区（其中包括，他与英格兰女王玛丽一世结婚后，对英格兰和爱尔兰短暂的统治）。腓力二世在位期间，西班牙开始进行全球殖民扩张，殖民地中就有菲律宾（以腓力二世名字命名的国家）。

28. 巴里·波森（1962年生），麻省理工学院政治学教授。他的研究专长为军事思想和外交政策之互动关系。

29. 利奥波德·冯·兰克（1795—1886），德意志历史学家。他是利用国家关系研究历史的先驱，兰克的这种研究方法在历史研究领域中很有影响力。

30. 罗纳德·里根（1911—2004），美国第四十任总统（1981—1989）。里根是共和党人，他在任期内领导美国打赢了冷战，曾大力推进民族主义和全球自由市场。

31. J. L. 理查德森，悉尼大学政府学讲师。

32. 弗里德里希·席勒（1759—1805），德意志博学者（在许多领域均有渊博的知识）。他是最早研究三十年战争的历史学家之一，但却因文学造诣而为世人所知。

33. 奥斯瓦德·施本格勒（1880—1936），德国历史学家。他著名的学术观点是：文明和生物一样，是有生命周期的。

34. 约瑟夫·斯大林（1878—1953），苏联共产党总书记（1922—1953年在任）。斯大林在任期间实施了严厉的经济政策和残酷的政治压迫行为，造成了数百万人死亡，但也使苏联一跃成为了超级大国。他的继任者尼基塔·赫鲁晓夫曾谴责他是一名暴君。

35. 詹尼斯·格罗斯·斯坦因（1943年生），加拿大多伦多大学蒙克全球事务学院政治学家。她的著作涉及很多话题，如外交、谈判和情报等。

36. A. J. P. 泰勒（1906—1990），英国历史学家。他主要研究十九和二十世纪政治外交史，经典之作为《第二次世界大战的起源》（1961）。

37. 哈里·S. 杜鲁门（1884—1972），第三十三任美国总统（1945—1953）。杜鲁门于冷战初期上台，主张采取"遏制"战略（杜鲁门主义）以削弱苏联的国际影响力。

38. **伊曼纽尔·沃勒斯坦**（1930—2019），美国社会学家、国际史学家。他是"世界系统"理论的提出者，他认为享有特权的"核心"国家（美国和欧洲）与无特权的"边缘化"国家（非洲、南美、南亚）之间的不平等经济交换构成了当今国际政治的主要特征。

39. **肯尼思·华尔兹**（1924—2013），美国国际关系学教授。华尔兹对现实主义进行了重构，让其更具科学面貌（通常被称为新现实主义）。新现实主义认为国家之间天生就是相互猜忌的，它们会通过权力平衡来确保自身的地位。该理论主导了20世纪70年代至90年代的国际关系研究。

40. **威廉·沃尔福斯**（1959年生），达特茅斯学院政府学教授。他特别强调安全和外交政策对一个国家的重要性。

41. **法里德·扎卡利亚**（1964年生），印度裔美国新闻记者、作家。他是《外交事务》和《时代》的期刊主编，出过专著《后美国世界》。他认为美国的重要性已有所下降，但这种情况不会给那些认为美国越来越无关紧要的国家带来危险。

WAYS IN TO THE TEXT

- The English historian Paul Kennedy, born in 1945, spent most of his career in the United States and achieved prominence toward the end of the Cold War* (a period of tension between the US and the communist Soviet Union* that began following World War II and ended with the collapse of European communism* in 1991).

- According to *The Rise and Fall of the Great Powers* (1987), powerful nations owe their dominance more to their economic strength than their military strength.

- The work made a very important argument that the United States may be vulnerable to decline in the future; the book's conclusions, however, continue to be debated.

Who Is Paul Kennedy?

The English historian Paul Kennedy, author of *The Rise and Fall of the Great Powers* (1987), was born in 1945 to a working-class family in the north of England. The first of his family to attend university, he graduated in history with first-class honors from Newcastle University.* He completed his doctorate at the University of Oxford* before moving to the United States to become chair in international history at Yale University.*

Rise and Fall, a book dealing with the politics of power at a time of great instability, was timely. It was published in 1987, just a few years before the end of the Cold War and the shift in the international balance of power that followed. During the Cold War, a period of heightened global tension, the United States and the Soviet Union (the USSR) engaged in covert operations, nuclear posturing, and proxy wars against one another, but the hostility never broke into open conflict. In the late 1980s, America had taken on a newly aggressive posture, and the Soviet Union stretched its budget to match the threat.

The book earned Kennedy a sort of academic and literary celebrity and saw him became a prolific commentator on global affairs. His scholarly work focused on the importance of international institutions (such as the United Nations).* His writing on great power politics found a home both in the general interest press and in journals aimed at foreign policy professionals such as *Foreign Affairs.**

What Does *The Rise and Fall of the Great Powers* Say?

In *Rise and Fall*, Kennedy argues that shifts in power around the globe follow a consistent pattern. Beginning with Europe in 1500, Kennedy looks at two dimensions of the predominant European power at the time, the Habsburg dynasty.* Members of this prosperous family of Austrian Spanish descent had managed to claim a range of powerful positions across Europe. Kennedy concludes that the Habsburgs lost power because their military commitments outpaced their economic prosperity. That is to say, they fought too many wars for their treasury to handle—a situation we might today call "imperial overreach." Diminished economic strength reduced their military strength, which in turn created more economic weakness.

So Kennedy sees factors like military strategy and the economy reinforcing the rise and the fall of great powers. He applies the same paradigm* (conceptual model) to the great powers in the centuries that followed: Spain, France, Britain, Germany, and the United States. Kennedy is not an "economic determinist". That is, he does not think underlying economic conditions predetermine the events of history. Instead, he believes the economic resources at their disposal give statesmen more or fewer options. Over time, more prosperous states—those with more options—remain more likely to prevail.

What made *Rise and Fall* such an important work was not its analysis of the sixteenth century. The work's later, predictive chapters applied those historical lessons to the great powers of the twentieth century. Kennedy predicted that the United States risked falling into the same pattern that had afflicted older empires. With its military commitments growing beyond its capacity to pay, America risked decline. During the 1990s, when the United States' leadership of the world appeared unchallenged, this assumption was not popular.

At the opening of the twenty-first century, the cracks in US predominance began to show. The terrorist attacks of September 11, 2001 ("9/11")* provoked the US into prolonged military occupations in the developing world; meanwhile, China began to claim an increasing share of world productivity. Following the global financial crisis of 2007–8, scholars began to reexamine Kennedy's question: was the United States in decline? American foreign policy entered an introspective phase. Should it increase its commitments abroad to combat rising powers? Should it decrease its commitments abroad to conserve a diminishing resource base?

The debate is far from over, and as it rages the world has only become more unstable and troubled.

Why Does *The Rise and Fall of the Great Powers* Matter?

While *Rise and Fall* offers a detailed survey of the events that have defined world history for the last 500 years, Kennedy sees history as more than a list of events. He seeks to *explain* events. What patterns can we uncover in historical events? What can we say about their causes? *Rise and Fall* helps readers understand *why* the events happened. The book serves as a key introduction to studies in both history and political science.

The work also offers readers a keen perspective on current affairs. Policymakers and pundits have long debated the question of whether or not the United States is facing decline. *Rise and Fall* suggests that the answer might be that it is. But it also argues that "declinism"*—the belief that one's nation is in irreversible decline—might be an oversimplification. Is it really just a matter of economics? Does "identity" matter? Is the role of global leader worth the struggle required?

Understanding how these two strands of thinking—large-scale historical analysis and the current-affairs perspective of "declinism"—compete requires critical thinking. Moreover, *Rise and Fall* helps readers understand the factors that make one school of thought more popular than another. Do the foundations of "declinism" hold up? The classic case of "imperial overreach" involves administering foreign territories where a country has security concerns. American foreign policy, both during and since the Cold War, has been a cause of concern for some thinkers (including Kennedy), who believe that the country's foreign adventures are imprudent.

Today, many voices argue that the US should follow some course or other in response to the actions of Syria, Russia, and so on. *Rise and Fall* introduces readers to the long-term consequences of the range of decisions: Intervene and risk overstretch; do not intervene and risk irrelevance. The work offers us a way to examine assertions that may include wild or unsupported assumptions.

SECTION 1
INFLUENCES

MODULE 1

THE AUTHOR AND THE
HISTORICAL CONTEXT

KEY POINTS

* *Rise and Fall* argues that a state's military predominance must be underpinned by prosperity relative to other states.

* Kennedy's study of history fostered a keen interest in the great empires (or more recently the international institutions) that govern the world.

* *Rise and Fall* appeared toward the end of the long period of global tension known as the Cold War, * when the United States stepped up its military commitments abroad under the "Reagan doctrine"*—an increase in military spending designed to pressure the Soviet Union.*

Why Read This Text?

Paul Kennedy's *The Rise and Fall of the Great Powers* is an epic exploration of history. His timeframe stretches from European dynastic* power struggles—struggles between aristocratic families for the right to rule—at the birth of the modern nation-state in 1500, up to the tail end of the Cold War.* The book was published in 1987; the Cold War ended with the collapse of the communist Soviet Union four years later. Rather than offering an account of history as a sequence of consecutive events, he explains how the underlying economic power of competing states produced grand battles and diplomatic intrigue.

States succeed *in relation to their competitors* when they preserve the most vibrant economy, pursue technological development, and avoid diverting too many resources to the military. But "Imperial overreach", may cause successful states to falter: their confidence grows as their strategic commitments grow, and with that, the size of their military; eventually the economy can no longer support the strategic commitments made by the political state, and the "Great Power" shrinks.

This book applies the same analytical method to all its subjects, whether Imperial Spain between the fifteenth and the nineteenth centuries, the British Empire, * or the modern United States.

> "[The United States will] contain and over time reverse Soviet expansionism by competing effectively on a sustained basis with the Soviet Union in all international arenas—particularly in the overall military balance and in geographical regions of priority concern to the United States."
>
> —— *United States National Security Decision Directive 75*, 1983

Author's Life

Paul Kennedy was born in the northern English city of Newcastle to a working-class family in 1945. In an interview with the English newspaper the *Guardian*, he said the family assumed that he would start working when he left school.[1] He surprised everyone, however, first when he went on to study history at Newcastle University, * and then when he sought an advanced degree, a DPhil at St. Antony's College* (an all-graduate college with a large

American population) at Oxford University. At Oxford, he worked under British military historian and strategist Sir Basil Liddell Hart.*

Growing up at the very end of the British Empire inspired Kennedy to write about "great powers, " and specifically to focus on what happens to those that engage in imperial overreach: Kennedy wondered if he might enter the imperial service, but "by the time I reached college [in 1963], almost all of that distant empire had become independent."[2] Finding it so unusual that a small island off the coast of Europe might govern a quarter of the world, he decided to study the phenomenon of the "great power."[3] In 1982, the United Kingdom and Argentina clashed over the Falkland Islands, small islands in the South Atlantic with a combined population of only a few thousand. Although the British won the Falklands War, * the conflict highlighted the extent to which the British have retreated from their overseas possessions.

Kennedy's academic career swiftly took him to Yale University* in the United States. While there, he published *Rise and Fall*—and the book catapulted him to academic superstardom. Soon he had been tapped as an advisor to both the United Nations* and the United States government. His work with the United Nations led him to write *The Parliament of Man*, a study of the role, shortcomings, and potential of the UN.[4] From empire to global governance, Kennedy writes about what he sees as the most important issues facing the world today.

Author's Background

A period of tension between the capitalist* United States and the communist* Soviet Union, the Cold War had defined international politics for nearly five decades beginning with the close of World War II.* (Capitalism is the economic and social system dominant in the Western world, in which industry is held in private hands; communism is a political ideology according to which property is held in common hands and the means of production—the tools and resources required for production—are administered by the state.)

While the Cold War did not involve direct conflict, it did produce proxy wars, such as the Korean War* (1950–3) and the Vietnam War* (1955–75), in which the United States fought the Soviet Union and China indirectly, and some terrifying near-wars such as the Cuban Missile Crisis* of 1962—an event that very nearly led to all-out nuclear conflict over the stationing of Soviet missiles in Cuba. In short, the Soviets and the Americans saw each other as existential threats. The possibility of nuclear destruction loomed large over the entire world.

Kennedy had originally planned to release *Rise and Fall* in 1986. If he had, the book would have dealt with great power dynamics only up to the end of World War II.*[5] But, having "started looking at the unbalanced fiscal policies and heavy military spending of the US and the USSR" in the late 1980s, he realized he needed to add these current events to the book and postponed its release for a year.[6]

The imbalances Kennedy mentioned stem in many ways from the "Reagan doctrine, " named for US president Ronald Reagan* and implemented with the aim of increasing pressure on the Soviet Union. An ideological hardliner, Reagan dubbed the Soviet Union the "evil empire" and called for a massive American arms build-up. He also channeled significantly increased support (in the form of arms, money, and training) to anti-Soviet groups plotting the overthrow of their communist-aligned governments around the world.[7]

By spending just a fraction more of its income on these strategic goals, the US intensified the pressure on an already strained Soviet domestic economy.[8] Soviet spending on its military, matching US commitments, consumed up to one-quarter of its total national income; it seemed unlikely that this state of affairs could be maintained.[9] In this period, with an internationally committed United States and a wobbling Soviet Union, Kennedy wrote his history of great power politics.

In certain ways, the historical patterns he had identified as far back as the 1500s still held true at the time he published the book. He had expected instability and violence to accompany the fall of any great power, but when the economically and militarily overcommitted government of the USSR fell, just four years after he published this book, the Cold War came to an unexpectedly quick and peaceful end by 1991. This outcome would have taken Kennedy by surprise, because he believed the fall of great powers was accompanied by military conflict, where the weakened great power would be defeated by the rising great power.

---

1. John Crace, "Paul Kennedy: Neocons' Worst Nightmare," *Guardian*, February 5, 2008, accessed September 3, 2015, http://www.theguardian.com/education/2008/feb/05/academicexperts. highereducationprofile.

2. Paul Kennedy, "The Imperial Mind: A Historian's Education in the Ways of Empire," *The Atlantic*, January 2008, accessed September 3, 2015, http://www.theatlantic.com/magazine/archive/2008/01/the-imperial-mind/306566/.

3. Kennedy, "The Imperial Mind."

4. Huw Richards, "Redrawing the Big Picture," *Times Higher Education*, August 28, 2008, accessed September 2, 2015, https://www. timeshighereducation.co.uk/features/redrawing-the-big-picture/403290. article.

5. Crace, "Paul Kennedy."

6. Crace, "Paul Kennedy."

7. Raymond L. Garthoff, *The Great Transition: American–Soviet Relations and the End of the Cold War* (Washington, DC: Brookings Institution, 1994), 8–9.

8. Garthoff, *The Great Transition*, 78.

9. Walter LaFeber, *America, Russia, and the Cold War, 1945–2002* (New York: McGraw Hill, 2002), 335.

ACADEMIC CONTEXT

KEY POINTS

- International history explains the present day at the international level through an analysis of the patterns of past events.

- While classical diplomatic history concerned itself with great men and large events, modern approaches to history examine underlying patterns; large events require explanation, and are not considered causes in themselves.

- Kennedy's focus on the economic foundations on which relationships between great powers are built reflects the work of his supervisors at Oxford, the British historians A. J. P. Taylor* and John Gallagher.*

The Work in Its Context

Paul Kennedy's *The Rise and Fall of the Great Powers* (1987) falls into the category of international history. Traditionally history has focused on "great men" and diplomatic relations between states—things to be explained. Modern approaches like Kennedy's focus on the underlying patterns of history—things doing the explaining. The eighteenth-century German historian Friedrich Schiller* articulated the discipline's statement of purpose in 1789. The international historian must "select from the stream of events those that exercise an essential, unmistakable, and easily comprehensible influence on the *present* shape of the world and the situation of the contemporary generation."[1]

We must also examine *Rise and Fall* in the context of the field of international relations.* Formerly a subset of historical studies, international relations became its own discipline in 1920 with the foundation of the first dedicated department at Aberystwyth University* in Wales. Rather than seeking to explain patterns in past events, the discipline "seeks to explain why international events occur the way they do."[2] So while international relations tends to be more interested in making a general theory of state action, the discipline of international history tends to focus more on explaining trends that extend beyond state borders. In practice, however, the division remains imperfect and they have more commonalities than differences.

> "In retrospect, though many were guilty, none was innocent. The purpose of political activity is to provide peace and prosperity; and in this every statesman failed, for whatever reason.This is a story without heroes, and perhaps even without villains."
>
> ——A. J. P. Taylor, *The Origins of the Second World War*

Overview of the Field

The practice of diplomacy became increasingly "professionalized" in Europe in the 1800s. At the same time, history became increasingly focused on explaining foreign policies and grand power politics.[3] Nineteenth-century German scholar Leopold von Ranke* was likely the first modern diplomatic historian. His concept of *Primat der Außenpolitik** (meaning, roughly, "the primacy of foreign policy") explained the history of Europe through external relationships between states. As he saw it, states "organize all [their] internal resources for the purpose of self-preservation" against threats posed by other states.[4] His work, including his famous *History of the Latin and Teutonic Peoples* (1824), [5] addresses the long-term roots of conflicts between entire societies as managed by great personalities. But perhaps the most important aspect of Ranke's work is that he relies on "real data" (especially diplomatic archives) to present the narrative of events as they truly happened.

Ranke's approach persisted until the middle of the twentieth century, when scholars began shift their focus. Instead of narrating history through the dramatic decisions and relationships of great men, they examined the underlying forces and the actions of common men. The influential French historian Fernand Braudel's* 1949 book, *The Mediterranean and the Mediterranean World in the Age of Philip II*, * illustrates this shift to "social" history.

Braudel examined Europe in the sixteenth century not through the thought-out diplomacy between "great men" (kings and generals), but by looking at the *longue durée**—the slow evolution of change. Braudel found these changes in geographic division, in the development of science and technology, and in economic matters. "Resounding events," Braudel wrote, "are often only momentary outbursts," and are only understandable in terms of "larger movements" underneath the surface.[6] Long-term history did not see diplomacy as explaining outcomes, but as one of the outcomes to be explained by sub-surface forces.

While the Annales school* of history with which Fernand Braudel was notably associated focused on *longue durée** history (that is, on the effects economic developments have had on historical outcomes), the twentieth-century American scholar Immanuel Wallerstein's* world systems analysis* aimed to show how the economic and social system of capitalism* formed the roots of a single international system. "In the late fifteenth and early sixteenth century," Wallerstein wrote, "there came into existence what we may call a European World Economy" as capitalism began to take root and expand.[7] This world economy gives us a kind of global division of labor: "core" states in Europe and North America engage in high-value production, extracting cheap labor and raw materials from the "periphery" colonialized or otherwise overpowered states in the global South. "Capitalism," argued Wallerstein, "as an economic mode is based on the fact that the economic factors operate within an arena larger than that which any political entity can totally control," which makes possible "the constant economic expansion of the world system."[8]

Academic Influences

Historians A. J. P. Taylor and John Andrew Gallagher, Kennedy's supervisors at Oxford, both studied the long-term diplomatic history of Britain. Taylor's 1954 work, *The Struggle for Mastery in Europe 1848–1918*, examined the diplomatic and economic origins of World War I.* The introduction to *Struggle* makes comparisons between great powers through the analysis of hard data concerning things such as manpower, coal output, and steel production to assess their genuine strength.[9] "The statesmen of Europe," Taylor pointed out, "looked at political appearances more than economic realities."[10] But Taylor primarily based his assessment of nineteenth-century power politics on diplomatic maneuvering. For example, he believed that the ambitiousness of German leadership, rather than some underlying material factor, caused World War I.

Kennedy's other academic mentor at Oxford was John Gallagher, a historian whose academic fame stemmed from a 1961 book he coauthored exploring British imperialism in Africa. *Africa and the Victorians:The Official Mind of Imperialism* reads more like theory than history. As Gallagher wrote, "We have not tried to write a history of the regions of Africa during the nineteenth century;" instead, Africa was "the hook on which we hang hypotheses about nationalism and world politics."[11] Once again, economy played a crucial role: "From Europe stemmed the economic drive to integrate" foreign regions as "markets and investment." Security played a secondary role, as the great powers tried to preempt others from expanding by increasing their own territorial footprint.[12]

It should be noted that Gallagher and Wallerstein (who argued that all states operate according to an economic system larger than any particular nation) differ in certain important respects. Gallagher argued that individual states secured foreign territory to support their enterprises abroad; for Wallerstein, all states played their parts in a larger system.

---

1. Friedrich Schiller, quoted in Gordon A. Craig, "The Historian and the Study of International Relations, "*American Historical Review* 88, no. 1 (1983): 3.

2. Tobjorn Knutsen, *History of International Relations Theory* (Manchester: Manchester University Press, 1997), 6.

3. Patrick Finney, "Introduction: What is International History?" in *Palgrave Advances in International History*, ed. Patrick Finney (Basingstoke: Palgrave Macmillan, 2005), 1.

4. Theodore H. von Laue, *Leopold Ranke, The Formative Years* (Princeton, NJ: Princeton University Press, 1950), 167.

5. Leopold von Ranke, *History of the Latin and Teutonic Peoples 1494–1514*, trans. G. R. Dennis (London: George Bell and Sons, 1909).

6. Fernand Braudel, *The Mediterranean and Mediterranean World in the Age of Philip II*, trans. Siân Reynolds (New York: Harper & Row, 1972), 21.

7. Immanuel Wallerstein, *The Modern World System I: Capitalist Agriculture and the Origins of the European World-Economy in the Sixteenth Century, with a New Prologue* (Berkeley: University of California Press, 2011), 15.

8. Wallerstein, *The Modern World System*, 348.

9. A. J. P. Taylor, *The Struggle for Mastery in Europe 1848–1918* (Oxford: Oxford University Press, 1969), xxvi–xxxiv.

10. Taylor, *Struggle for Mastery*, xxxii.

11. Ronald Robinson et al., *Africa and the Victorians: The Official Mind of Imperialism* (Basingstoke: Macmillan, 1981), xxv.

12. Robinson et al., *Africa and the Victorians*, 485.

THE PROBLEM

KEY POINTS

* Scholars were asking the question: when looking at the politics of the most powerful states, what forces explain the broad patterns of history?
* Two broad approaches dominated: scholars of international relations emphasized structural factors; scholars concerned with "great men" emphasized individual decisions.
* Looking at a longer arc of history than his contemporaries, Kennedy focused on both structural trends *and* individual responses.

Core Question

Paul Kennedy's *The Rise and Fall of the Great Powers* (1987) is relevant to a question that political theorists and historians had already been considering for many years when the book was published: what is the nature of the underlying forces driving political outcomes?

Explanations of political events and theories of statecraft developed according to the methods of *longue durée** ("long term") analysis (an approach taken by historians of the Annales school, * who were concerned with historical—often social—changes over the long term) had been being made for more than a century. Theorists looked to identify underlying forces in order to predict future outcomes; historians looked to identify the underlying forces to explain past events.

The perilous nuclear standoff between the United States and the Soviet Union* and their allies that defined the Cold War, * however, made it more essential than ever to answer this important question. With both sides possessing nuclear weapons, predicting the outcome of this tense period seemed to be literally a matter of life and death. It was particularly urgent that scholars and politicians should come to understand the present through the lessons of the past—the purpose of the study of international relations since the discipline's inception.

Moreover, the great powers had become more interdependent by the end of World War II* than other great powers had been in the past. For Kennedy, the "large powers"—the United States, the USSR, * China, Japan, and the European community—were required to manage and exercise their economic and military power in such a way that they would not overexert it and sow the seeds of their own decline.[1]

> "History, as anyone who has spent any time at all studying it would surely know, has a habit of making bad prophets out of both those who make and those who chronicle it."
>
> ——John Lewis Gaddis, "The Long Peace"

The Participants

One of the other key perspectives on great power politics came from twentieth-century American political scientist Kenneth Waltz.* His *Theory of International Politics*, published in 1979, presented an entirely theory-driven (that is, non-historical) picture of global politics.Waltz believed the particular "goings on" of individual states remained entirely incidental to the course of history. After all, war has always been an outcome of relationships between great powers, regardless of how states are governed or by whom.[2] Waltz's theory was that, since the international sphere was anarchic* (that is, it was ungoverned), states must look after their own security. From this perspective, all states have the same interest (survival) and the same (military) means to ensure it.[3] We can only compare states on the basis of their power.

Waltz often compares states to billiard balls, which differ only in size and weight; for him, states differ only in their material capabilities. History, then, merely recounts the outcome of the balance of power. Following his theory into the present day of the 1970s, Waltz believed that the enemy states of the Soviet Union and the United States would never fight because the risk was too great.While both were powerful, neither was powerful enough to prevail. International relations scholars call this the stable condition of bipolarity.*

Kennedy's colleague at Yale, the American historian John Lewis Gaddis, * presented a different answer: for him, "if the structure of bipolarity in itself encouraged stability, so too did certain inherent characteristics of the bilateral Soviet–American relationship."[4] Just as the balance of power mattered, so did the players in this balance. Gaddis sought to explain why the relationship between the Soviet Union and the United States— though certainly not friendly—remained so stable. He believes that the superpowers* (politically, militarily, and economically dominant nations) could maintain peace so long as they followed certain patterns of behavior:

- respecting one another's spheres of influence* (the areas in which they wield special authority),
- avoiding military confrontation,
- avoiding nuclear confrontation,
- accepting injustice so long as it is predictable (that is, injustice that would not come as a surprise or provoke a response—for example, the existence of political prisoners was accepted),
- avoiding interference in one another's domestic politics.[5]

Gaddis explains the historical outcome of "stability" by examining the choices made by the superpowers rather than the nature of the superpowers themselves.

The Contemporary Debate

Kennedy's line of inquiry remained uniquely ambitious for his time. He never directly comments on either Waltz's or Gaddis's visions of history. But to make some broad generalizations, Kennedy differed from Waltz because he delved into the particular, and from Gaddis because he aimed for the generalizable: "Precisely because neither economic historians nor military historians had entered this field, the story [of the grand history of all great powers] had simply suffered from neglect."[6]

Essentially, Kennedy saw work in the fields of international relations and history—even studies sometimes described as "big" history, which offer explanations of all of human history with reference to some single factor—as suffering from a blind spot. They did not focus on the *longue durée* history of great powers as a phenomenon. Gaddis focused on a particular great power or group of great powers; Waltz focused on power in general. "What most readers and listeners wanted, " Kennedy suggested, "was *more* detail, *more* coverage of the background, simply because there was no study available."[7]

Kennedy liked to paraphrase the nineteenth-century German statesman Otto von Bismarck:* "all of these Powers are traveling on 'the stream of Time, ' which they can 'neither create nor direct, ' but upon which they can 'steer with more or less skill and experience.'"[8] Kennedy's theory formed the middle way between the international relations theorist and the historian.

---

1. Paul Kennedy, *The Rise and Fall of the Great Powers* (New York: Vintage Books, 1989), 540.

2. Kenneth Waltz, *Theory of International Politics* (Reading: Addison Wesley, 1979), 65.

3. Waltz, *Theory*, 99.

4. John Lewis Gaddis, "The Long Peace: Elements of Stability in the Postwar International System," *International Security* 10, no. 4 (1986): 110.

5. Gaddis, "The Long Peace, " 133–8.

6. Kennedy, *Rise and Fall*, xxv.

7. Kennedy, *Rise and Fall*, xxv.

8. Kennedy, *Rise and Fall,* 540.

MODULE 4
THE AUTHOR'S CONTRIBUTION

KEY POINTS

* Kennedy aimed to present a history of powerful European states from 1500 to the late twentieth century.

* He surveyed political and economic data from 1500 onward, but avoided making predictions or creating a theory.

* The roots of *Rise and Fall* can be found in debates between the German historian Oswald Spengler* and the Canadian American historian William McNeill.* While they were not contemporaries, both made arguments about the ultimate future of the West.

Author's Aims

Paul Kennedy opens *The Rise and Fall of the Great Powers* with an unambiguous statement of intent. He says he aims "to trace and explain how the various Great Powers have risen and fallen, relative to each other, " in terms of power, influence, and global importance, "over the five centuries, " in Europe.[1]

Why five centuries? Why only Europe? After all, there have been "great powers" outside this time period, such as the Roman Empire.* There have also been non-European great powers, such as China during the Ming Dynasty* of 1368–1644, but Kennedy does not concern himself with these. He chose to begin with the year 1500, he notes, because it marked the beginning of the "transoceanic, global system of states."And he chose to center his study on Europe, because the states on that continent would come to define the way in which that transoceanic global system worked.[2]

Kennedy makes much of Europe's peculiar geography in explaining why Europe eventually became the "center of the world," politically speaking. Rivers, mountains, and forests divide the territories of Europe. These natural demarcations led to the natural emergence of many centers of power and these centers would vie for dominance. In this competitive system, the societies most able to fight and rule would prevail.[3]

Military might was not the only factor, but it was certainly the most important. After the voyage of the Italian explorer Columbus* in 1492 opened up the possibility of conquest abroad, Europe pulled ahead materially from other societies. A Spanish Austrian family—the Habsburgs*—threatened to become the predominant power in Europe; a coalition of European states dashed these hopes after a full 150 years of intermittent fighting.[4] Importantly, the Habsburg Dynasty was not a state but a family whose alliances gave it hereditary control over a range of constantly shifting areas of Europe. Still, whether soldiers shed their blood for a state or for a family—whether they were fighting for territory or fighting to uphold personal bonds of loyalty—the war carried the same human and economic costs.

> *"The problem which historians—as opposed to political scientists—have in grappling with general theories is that the evidence of the past is almost always too varied to allow for 'hard' scientific conclusions."*
> —— Paul Kennedy, *The Rise and Fall of the Great Powers*

Approach

Kennedy's approach embraces a wide range of information and techniques of looking at information. *Rise and Fall* "concerns itself a great deal with wars ... but it is not strictly a book about military history."At the same time, while it is concerned with the evolution of the global economy, it is equally "not a work of economic history."[5] It gives us a synthesis of the actions of statesmen and the (economic) forces they brought to bear in working with (and against) one another.

Kennedy notes that a historian might understand his approach as "a broad and yet reasonably detailed survey" of great power politics, explained with reference to slow economic and technological changes. A political scientist might read the book as an exercise in theory-making—the theory being that we can predict the performance of great powers by looking at economic trends. But Kennedy is suspicious of such activity. Rather than making a predictive theory, he aims at "making sense of " past events. To put it crudely, money does not necessarily equal success, but "the power position of the leading nations has closely paralleled their relative economic position over the past five centuries." Kennedy believes it might be worthwhile to speculate how this could play out in future—but he hesitates to offer a prediction or make any claims to scientific precision.[6]

Contribution in Context

Kennedy was hardly alone in trying to write a "big" history of the West. In his 1922 book *The Decline of the West*, the German historian Oswald Spengler asked, "Is there a logic of history?"[7] Spengler argued that we should use "cultures" (such as the West) to analyze history, and we should see those cultures as having natural life cycles, from birth to death. Spengler defined cultures by the "prime symbols" that represent their main project. In his view, the "symbol" for Western culture is the character of Dr. Faustus, * a figure from German folklore dating back to at least the sixteenth century; according to the story, Faustus sold his soul to the devil in return for unlimited knowledge.Western society is "Faustian" because humanity has sold its soul and connection to the land for technical sophistication and industrial production. Cultures, over time, become civilizations, and increasingly focus on outward expansion. Spengler associates civilization with decline, since civilization represents the moment when the culture stops innovating and turns instead to expansion.

In response to Spengler's cyclical, pessimistic view, twentieth-century Canadian American historian William McNeill wrote *The Rise of the West*. In this 1962 work, McNeill argued that we should not see history as a series of cycles that different cultures progress through independently. Instead, "the principal factor promoting historically significant social change is contact with strangers possessing new and unfamiliar skills." As he sees it, civilization in general—and Western civilization in particular—possesses a uniquely high concentration of skills.[8] Civilizations remain separate, but the exchanges between them define their life cycles.

Taking a view almost entirely opposite to Spengler, McNeill

believed that the West assured its dominance when it gained seafaring technology.This enabled the nations of Europe to become infinitely expansionist:"the result was to link the Atlantic face of Europe with the shores of most of the Earth." Europe "won" because it could adopt technologies and resources from everyone else at the expense of every other region.[9]

Both Spengler and McNeill focused on the relative position of the West with regard to other regions, telling a story of "rise and fall" similar to Kennedy's. Kennedy based his work on more ideas, however, with a focus on factors like technology or geography.

1. Paul Kennedy, *The Rise and Fall of the Great Powers* (New York: Vintage Books, 1989), xv.
2. Kennedy, *Rise and Fall*, xv.
3. Kennedy, *Rise and Fall*, 30.
4. Kennedy, *Rise and Fall*, 31.
5. Kennedy, *Rise and Fall*, xv.
6. Kennedy, *Rise and Fall*, xxiv.
7. Oswald Spengler, *The Decline of the West*, ed. Helmut Warner, trans. Charles F. Atkinson (Oxford: Oxford University Press, 1991), 3.
8. William McNeill, "*The Rise of the West* After Twenty-five Years, " *Journal of World History* 1, no. 1 (1990): 2.
9. William McNeill, *The Rise of the West: A History of the Human Community* (Chicago: Chicago University Press, 1991), 564–5.

SECTION 2
IDEAS

MAIN IDEAS

KEY POINTS

* While no one has created a formal definition of a "great power," the term commonly denotes a state recognized by its peers as capable of holding its own against any other in a military contest.

* Great powers fall when their military commitments exceed their productive capacity. Great powers rise when they build their military and productive capacity relative to those of other states.

* Although *Rise and Fall* contains no complex mathematics or academic jargon, its length can intimidate some readers.

Key Themes

At heart, Paul Kennedy's *The Rise and Fall of the Great Powers* aims to answer the question of what makes a state a "great power." We may define the term in two ways. The simple definition holds that a great power is a state that can reasonably defeat any other power in combat; the more social definition holds that a great power is a state that other states recognize as a great power. So the status of "great power" remains more a matter of mutual recognition than the passing of some arbitrary threshold.

The "great powers" Kennedy concerns himself with are, initially, dynasties centered on Spain, France, and Austria. Later in the book, he examines new entrants to the "Great Power Club"— including Russia, Great Britain, and Germany, among others.

For Kennedy, "all of the major shifts in the world's military-power balances"—meaning the relative strength of sovereign states—"have followed alterations in the productive balances."[1] While his conclusion appears to be that victory follows wealth, it is not so simple; great powers make mistakes, even if they have significant resources. More often than not, then, great power conflicts can be prolonged and bloody, even if victory usually goes to the more prosperous of the two powers in conflict.

> "While it would be quite wrong ... to claim that the outcome of the First World War was predetermined, the evidence presented here suggests that the overall course of that conflict—the early stalemate between the two sides, the ineffectiveness of the Italian entry, the slow exhaustion of Russia, the decisiveness of American intervention ... correlates closely with the economic and industrial production and effectively mobilized forces available to each alliance during the different phases of the struggle."
> —— Paul Kennedy, *The Rise and Fall of the Great Powers*

Exploring the Ideas

The first "rise and fall" Kennedy discusses is that of the Habsburg Empire, whose story unfolds between 1516 and 1689. In 1516, the Habsburg Dynasty celebrated the coronation of Charles as Carlos I, King of Spain. But through his ancestors, he was also Charles V, * leader of the Holy Roman Empire*—a political body that encompassed large parts of Austria, the Netherlands, Naples, and other territories around Europe. This "empire" was not a centralized authority like a state; it remained an association of distant provinces ruled by a single family.

Looking at why the Habsburgs failed, Kennedy argues that despite the enormous wealth from their holdings in Europe and the New World (Spain's territories in South America), the Habsburgs could not afford to fight wars on many fronts over 140 years. They built their own warships rather than use trade ships, they maintained internal and external trade barriers, and they expelled Jews from their territories.[2] In short, the Habsburgs failed "to recognize the importance of preserving the economic underpinnings of a powerful military machine."

This revealed to Kennedy an important lesson:"the manufacturer and the farmer were as important as the cavalry officer and the pikeman."[3] A state must maintain enough productive capacity to fund its military commitments.

A great power fell, then, as a consequence of neglecting financial matters. In its wake, five great powers arose: Great Britain, the remains of the Habsburg Empire (Austria-Hungary), Prussia (a territory today incorporated into northern Germany), France, and Russia mounted the stage. Kennedy points to the "military revolution" of the time, as European states equipped, paid, and directed large, professional standing volunteer armies in Europe.[4]

Geography and finance, Kennedy writes, are factors of comparable importance.[5] Maintaining a professional army in peacetime required the state to borrow from financial markets. And great powers had to consider all the possible geographic fronts from which an invader could launch an attack. Given these circumstances, states that raised extensive funds to become "great powers" and fight one another fanned the flames of their own growth, pumping money into their own industries to house, equip, and train their military.

The historian John Brewer* calls this phenomenon the "fiscal-military state" and notes its characteristics as "high taxes, a growing and well-organized civil administration, a standing army, and the determination to act as a major ... power."[6] In essence, the strongest fiscal position supports the strongest military position. As Kennedy puts it, no battlefield blunder was "enough to cancel out the advantages which that [combatant] possessed in terms of trained manpower, supply, organization, and economic base."[7]

This logic pervades Kennedy's exploration of history. As he points out in his assessment of World War I* (1914–18), the victorious powers enjoyed "a marked superiority in productive forces" after the United States joined the war in 1917. This "marked superiority, " however, does not only reflect the quantity of available resources; it also reflects how those resources get deployed.

Kennedy discusses Germany's Hindenburg Programme, * a program intended to double the production of munitions. Germany made a "massive infrastructural investment" in new industrial resources such as blast furnaces for gun-making. But accomplishing this required the country to redirect all of its skilled labor, and to allow its other industrial and agricultural output to succumb to chronic neglect.[8] In the end, Germany's loss stemmed as much from neglecting its economic diversity as it did from any external military force.

Similarly, Kennedy's account of the end of World War II* shows that the "middle powers" (Britain, France, Germany) exhausted themselves, both by maintaining far-flung empires and by engaging in a grinding total war against one another. They followed this well-worn path to decline, [9] leaving the Americans and the Russians as the world's two dominant opposing powers.

Language and Expression

While Kennedy's subject, not to mention the length of the book, may be intimidating for some readers, his prose is clear and free of jargon. He illustrates his argument with tables such as that comparing the money spent on armaments between 1940 and 1943 and the money spent on either side of World War II. The simple charts supplement the text itself; the reader does not need to do any mathematics.[10]

Kennedy organizes his book chronologically, devoting much of the book to an overview of military actions (including wars lasting over a century) and economic and technological developments.These things actually constitute the "stuff " of history—the events we seek to explain.

Finally, he offers much more explanation and many more examples in the appendices; the reader will do well to follow each chapter through its endnotes, where he places many illustrative quotes from historical figures and useful bibliographic information.

---

1. Paul Kennedy, *The Rise and Fall of the Great Powers* (New York: Vintage Books, 1989), 439.

2. Kennedy, *Rise and Fall*, 55.

3. Kennedy, *Rise and Fall*, 72.

4. M. Roberts, "The Military Revolution, 1560–1600, " in *Essays in Swedish History*, ed. M. Roberts (London: Weidenfeld & Nicolson, 1967), 217.

5. Kennedy, *Rise and Fall*, 76.

6. John Brewer, *The Sinews of Power: War, Money, and the English State 1688–1783* (London: Century Hutchinson, 1988), 137.

7. Kennedy, *Rise and Fall*, 192.

8. Kennedy, *Rise and Fall*, 270.

9. Kennedy, *Rise and Fall*, 366–7.

10. Kennedy, *Rise and Fall*, 335.

MODULE 6
SECONDARY IDEAS

KEY POINTS

* The shifting balances between the great powers of the sixteenth to twentieth centuries set the stage for a new kind of competition in the second half of the twentieth century.
* The Cold War* was defined by its two opposing poles led by the United States and the Soviet Union, * the competing ideologies of communism* and capitalism, * and the threat of nuclear war—but its underlying dynamics remained economic.
* Kennedy's argument that the United States was in decline rested on the premise that the country's global commitments outmatched its capability to meet them; critics did not universally accept this viewpoint.

Other Ideas

In *The Rise and Fall of the Great Powers*, Paul Kennedy both explores the dynamics underlying the shifting balance of powers at the international level and, importantly, examines the roots of the international system of the twentieth century. The book's second major argument is that the dynamic of uneven economic growth "has had crucial long-term impacts" on the modern state system.[1]

The twentieth-century system was the result of two world wars that themselves resulted from jockeying for power among the five great powers of the eighteenth and nineteenth centuries. "It was becoming clear [in the aftermath of World War II]* that the global balance of power ... would be totally different from that preceding it."[2] France, Italy, and Germany were decimated by war; Japan (the first non-European great power) had lost its bid for mastery of Asia. Even the United Kingdom, which emerged from the war relatively better off than its European neighbors, could not compete with the rising powers of the United States and the Soviet Union.

In addition to exploring the roots and dynamics of the multipolar* international system in Europe (a system in which many nations were competing for supremacy), Kennedy discusses how these dynamics resulted in the emergence of the bipolar* international system between 1945 and 1991 (a system in which two nations vied for dominance). But Kennedy remains most interested in discussing how the US—in its Cold War bipolar contest with Russia from 1945 to 1991 and after—may follow old patterns and find itself in decline.

"It was the United States alone which at this time had the productive and technological resources not only to wage two large-scale conventional wars but also to invest the scientists, raw materials, and money (about $2 billion) in the development of a new weapon [the atomic bomb] which might or might not work. The devastation inflicted upon Hiroshima, together with Berlin's fall into the hands of the Red Army, not only symbolized the end of another war, it also marked the beginning of a new order in world affairs."
—— Paul Kennedy, The Rise and Fall of the Great Powers

Exploring the Ideas

The end of World War II in 1945 left the Soviet Union and the

United States facing one another in Europe. Joseph Stalin, * the General Secretary of the Soviet Communist Party (the Soviet Union's highest political office), consolidated control over Eastern Europe. He also pushed his armies into Central Asia, while "maintaining a high level of military security ... to deter future aggressors" and keep its future conquests from falling into the American sphere of influence.*[3] In contrast, the United States attempted to enjoy what it called a global "Pax Americana."* Although the term refers to peace and prosperity under American rule, it disguises a great deal of internal violence in developing countries of the southern hemisphere. Kennedy believes the term references the "Pax Britannica"* of the late nineteenth century, a time of relative stability when Britain's "productive power and world influence" were predominant.[4] But two things made this twentieth-century global contest between great powers fundamentally different from its predecessors: the role of ideology and nuclear weapons.

Both blocs remained committed to their respective ideologies. The United States and its allies espoused capitalism (a system in which personal liberty is valued, elections are held, and industry and resources are held in private hands); the Soviet Union and its satellites practiced communism* (a system in which citizens are expected to be obedient to the state, which owns and manages industry and resources and in which property is held in common). Harry S.Truman, * president of the United States between 1945 and 1953, declared that "the United States ... [helps] free people to maintain their institutions and their integrity against aggressive

movements that seek to impose upon them totalitarian* regimes."
In other words, he vowed to prevent Soviet communism from
expanding to new countries.[5]

In earlier eras, states would fight on a religious basis, or
for abstract "national interests." But the Cold War antagonists
genuinely saw international affairs as a global struggle between
good and evil and unlike previous great power standoffs, the entire
world had a stake in the outcome of this one as the great powers
had amassed arsenals of nuclear weapons.[6] Both the United States
and Soviet Union had the means to eradicate all life on Earth at the
push of a button.

Grand rhetoric—language intended to persuade or inflame—
surrounded the Cold War. Kennedy's analysis of the conflict rests
on the same logic as his analyses of previous great power struggles.
It comes down to industry and economy rather than military. In the
course of the Cold War, it became clear that the USSR's military
and nuclear prowess "was not matched by parallel achievements
at the economic level, " especially in terms of technological
innovation.[7] Kennedy hesitates to predict the future of international
politics (in doing so he would leave history and enter the realm of
political theory) but he does reiterate that "without a rough balance
between these competing demands of defense, consumption, and
investment, a Great Power is unlikely to preserve its status for
long."[8]

Overlooked

After Kennedy had substantially completed the book, he decided to add some chapters dealing with the modern-day United States. The argument he makes in this section, which does not necessarily pertain to his main theory, has been perhaps the *most* discussed portion of the book: the United States, he reasons, is in relative decline. The US, like "Imperial Spain around 1600 or the British Empire around 1900, " must deal with foreign military commitments that it has made in previous decades.[9]

Kennedy suggests that the United States may run the risk of imperial overreach; "decision-makers in Washington must face the awkward and enduring fact that the sum total of the United States' global interests and obligations is nowadays far larger than the country's power to defend them all simultaneously."[10] For Kennedy, American decline would be analogous to British decline in the nineteenth century.

Kennedy notes that declining *relative* economic performance underpins this overreach. While the United States carried less debt than it had relative to the rest of the world at the end of World War II, the country's Gross National Product* or GNP (the market value of all goods and services produced in one year by the residents of a country) and its manufacturing and agricultural output were declining.[11] Yet, simultaneously, US commitments abroad increased, with a corresponding pressure on the nation to spend more on its military.

While critics did not exactly overlook this argument, it was not central to Kennedy's project. One early critic—the American conservative political analyst Samuel Huntington*—believes Kennedy's theory that imperial overreach leads to decline may be true. But Huntington does not believe this necessarily applies to the US. For him, Kennedy's declinist* thesis rests too strongly on the assumption that economic power comes from similar sources. Huntington believes "the central sources of American strength" are competition through capitalism, social mobility, and renewal of culture and thought through immigration and universities. Kennedy, he believes, sees strength as coming from simple productive power measured in bushels of wheat or industrial output.[12]

1. Paul Kennedy, *The Rise and Fall of the Great Powers* (New York: Vintage Books, 1989), 439.
2. Kennedy, *Rise and Fall*, 357.
3. Kennedy, *Rise and Fall*, 363.
4. Kennedy, *Rise and Fall*, 192.
5. Kennedy, *Rise and Fall*, 372.
6. Kennedy, *Rise and Fall*, 370.
7. Kennedy, *Rise and Fall*, 429.
8. Kennedy, *Rise and Fall*, 446.
9. Kennedy, *Rise and Fall*, 515.
10. Kennedy, *Rise and Fall*, 515.
11. Kennedy, *Rise and Fall*, 529.
12. Samuel Huntington, "The US: Decline or Renewal?" *Foreign Affairs* 67, no. 2 (1988): 89.

ACHIEVEMENT

KEY POINTS

* Some critics questioned Kennedy's theories on the relationship between economics and power. They believe that by focusing on one factor alone, he lost the ability to explain outcomes that resulted from other factors.

* While *Rise and Fall* did not offer any predictions of how the Cold War* would end, overreach certainly played a role; the idea that something similar might happen to the United States in the future struck a nerve.

* Critics believe Kennedy's analysis was limited because his assumptions applied to European states; for them, he excluded non-European states from great power status by holding them to standards defined by Europe.

Assessing the Argument

Considering Paul Kennedy's *The Rise and Fall of the Great Powers*, certain questions remain difficult to answer. For example: does the book provide a useful explanatory model for understanding the peculiar history of "great power politics"? Does it explain why events unfolded the way they unfolded, without straying into the realm of prediction?

Although the Australian academic J. L. Richardson* thinks Kennedy's unwillingness to predict is "commendably modest and open ended, " he finds his conclusions to be "disappointingly meagre." Richardson notes that Kennedy does not explain how states form coalitions, or how they identify their friends and enemies.[1] Second, Richardson recognizes that Kennedy has done great work analyzing the relationship between economic growth and war but he feels Kennedy did not necessarily finish his argument. "The economically strongest coalition wins," Richardson writes, admittedly oversimplifying Kennedy's conclusion. "[B]ut why were there particular coalitions formed in the first place? Why did great wars take place when they did, while at other times wars remained limited or were avoided altogether? ... Kennedy's work provokes questions of this kind but offers little to answer them."[2]

Essentially, Richardson's critique is that Kennedy can explain history only as it happened. He cannot account for wars averted, only wars that were waged. Are we left with a "history of great power politics, " or a device that merely explains wars in which great powers have engaged? For Richardson, the work suffers by treating individual statesmen as relatively unimportant "relevant units of analysis, " compared to broad-based economic, strategic, administrative, and technical shifts.[3]

> "The end of the Cold War brought about nothing less than the collapse of an international system, something that has happened in modern history only once before."
> ——John Lewis Gaddis, "International Relations Theory and the End of the Cold War"

Achievement in Context

Rise and Fall was published in 1987. According to Kennedy's Yale colleague John Lewis Gaddis, * a notable historian in his own right, the work seized the American national consciousness because it highlighted that "the condition of being a great power is in fact transitory, " and may prove transitory for the United States as well.[4] Moreover, Kennedy suggested that the Cold War's end would not be peaceful. Gaddis cites Kennedy's conclusion: war has always accompanied the collapse of a great power empire, and those "who rejoice at the present-day difficulties of the Soviet Union* and who look forward to the collapse of that empire might wish to recall that such transformations normally occur at very great cost."[5]

But in this case, history did not repeat itself. The end of the Cold War and collapse of the Soviet Union occurred in relative peace.The Warsaw Pact*—the treaty of cooperation that had bound communist states together—officially dissolved in 1989. Lacking the guarantee of Soviet support against uprisings, communist leaders across Eastern Europe found themselves deposed in rapid sequence.This left the United States as the only surviving great power.

While Kennedy did not predict *how* the Cold War would end, he did understand that it would end. And according to one popular strand of thinking, its end did seem to mirror Kennedy's theory: by increasing defense spending in the United States, Ronald Reagan* (president between 1981 and 1989) forced the Soviet Union to make unsustainably large expenditures on its own military. The Soviets had also overextended themselves with overseas military commitments. These factors undermined the Soviet economy's ability to sustain itself. But we should note that Reagan's military spending did raise the US national deficit (the difference between its spending and its income) at the expense of the kind of "productive base" Kennedy believes is important.[6]

Some scholars disagree with this assessment, however. The American political scientist Richard Ned Lebow* and the Canadian international relations expert Janice Gross Stein* believe the arms build-up prolonged the Cold War. In their view, the conflict only ended once the leaders of the United States and Soviet Union met face to face and learned to trust one another as people.[7]

Limitations

The British historian Jeremy Black* suggests a difficulty with Kennedy's approach to the discipline, finding the same challenge with other Western historians who work on a "grand" level; for him, the issue of identifying great powers is problematic.

Scholars usually define "great powers" as those that have a significant amount of industrial and financial power. Still, as in many exclusive clubs, a state cannot be admitted to the "great power" club unless other members recognize it as one of their own. Black argues that, by definition, this excludes non-Western states; indeed, the list of attributes required for a state to be a "great power" merely describes certain Western states."Thus, Japan, and then China, in the twentieth century are considered" great powers, but only because they merit the definition on Western terms—"earlier they are ruled out."[8] In other words, anyone can play the great power game, but the West makes the rules.

Black believes other powers outside Europe—such as the

thirteenth-century Eurasian Mongol Empire*—would have been considered great powers if Kennedy had not loaded his premises in favor of European states. Black suggests other possible measures of great power status, such as honor and prestige— even if unconnected to financial or military resources. Without considerations like honor, Black writes, "it is difficult to explain why Austria, which he refers to as becoming a 'marginal first-class power' ... from the eighteenth century" continued to receive such status, given its relative lack of material resources.[9]

1. J. L. Richardson, "Paul Kennedy and International Relations Theory: A Comparison with Robert Gilpin, " *Australian Journal of International Affairs* 45, no. 1 (1991): 75.

2. Richardson, "Paul Kennedy and International Relations Theory, " 76.

3. Richardson, "Paul Kennedy and International Relations Theory, " 76.

4. John Lewis Gaddis, "International Relations Theory and the End of the Cold War, " *International Security* 17, no. 3 (1992): 50–1.

5. Paul Kennedy, *The Rise and Fall of the Great Powers* (New York: Vintage Books, 1989), 514.

6. Richard Ned Lebow and Janice Gross Stein, "Reagan and the Russians, " *Atlantic Monthly*, February 1994, accessed September 12, 2015, http:// www.theatlantic.com/past/politics/foreign/reagrus.htm.

7. Lebow and Stein, "Reagan and the Russians."

8. Jeremy Black, *Great Powers and the Quest for Hegemony: The World Order Since 1500*, (London: Routledge, 2008), 1–2.

9. Black, *Great Powers and the Quest for Hegemony*, 20.

MODULE 8
PLACE IN THE AUTHOR'S WORK

KEY POINTS

* *Rise and Fall* served as the culmination of Kennedy's career looking at grand diplomatic history.

* Kennedy focused his work initially on high politics, and later on global governance.

* *Rise and Fall* remains most famous for its discussion of American decline; for this reason, Kennedy remains an influential academic and popular figure.

Positioning

The Rise and Fall of the Great Powers was not Paul Kennedy's first significant book—or even his first to be titled *Rise and Fall*. Kennedy called his first prominent work, published in 1976, *The Rise and Fall of British Naval Mastery*. This reflects his early fascination with ways in which the British Empire* balanced its power on land and sea. In his later work, Kennedy would continue to explore one key element of *British Naval Mastery*: Britain's global influence and prosperity did not stem from the strength of its navy. In fact, the relationship ran the other way around.[1] Britain's domestic economy remains crucial to its ability to project its force at sea.

Kennedy published another similarly titled and significant work, *The Rise of the Anglo-German Antagonism: 1860–1914*, in 1980. Like Kennedy's other books, *Antagonism* dealt with all levels of political life, especially international diplomacy and domestic politics. In it, as in his other works, he advances the theory that "the most profound cause [of Anglo-German tension] ... was economic."[2] Germany's political unification and economic growth in the nineteenth century indicated that the nation was heading towards socialism* (a political system in which industry and resources are held in the hands of the people), especially as elements of the population campaigned to make domestic politics more democratic. The ruling elite responded with a strategy called *Weltpolitik*, * which aimed at fostering intense national pride and increasing German military power to make it a great power, like its neighbors France and Russia. Essentially, *Weltpolitik* ("world policy") is tough diplomacy, in which a risen Germany, having attained parity with its European neighbors, seeks to install itself as a "great power" with an empire, a strong navy, and tough-talking diplomacy.

> " *If the immediate fallout was hard to deal with, the longer-term consequences have proved positive. The book became an international bestseller and has been translated into 23 languages; only last year the Chinese issued a reprint to coincide with a new 10-part TV series based on it.*"
> ——John Crace, "Paul Kennedy: Neocons' Worst Nightmare, " *The Guardian*

Integration

Kennedy's early body of work remains relatively well integrated. By the time *Rise and Fall* appeared in 1987, scholars had written a great deal about how economic prosperity (or lack thereof) connected to political outcomes. After *Rise and Fall*, Kennedy branched out, expanding both his subject and his purpose.

In 1993's *Preparing for the 21st Century*, Kennedy examines transnational forces—rather than the "nation-state"—as the main unit of analysis. He expects that population growth, resource scarcity, environmental damage, and a globally widening wealth-gap will fundamentally undermine the power of the nation-state. For him, the nation-state was a European institution, and too insular to deal with global problems.[3] The only way to deal with these interlocking problems, he maintains, is to make leadership more transnational.

In *The Parliament of Man*, published in 2006, Kennedy continues the pessimistic discussion he began in *Preparing*. But this time he has a solution in mind: the United Nations, * a global institution founded to promote cooperation between nations. True, the United Nations has problems of its own. It cannot create authoritative rules, and it still largely respects the sovereignty of nation-states but in theory the UN provides humanity's best chance of coordinating a genuine global response to transnational problems that defy national solutions. The American international relations scholar John Ikenberry* writes that in *Parliament of Man* Kennedy focuses on how the UN's role in "supporting social and political advancements" or "peacekeeping and the promotion of human rights" has produced some success. Humanity has a fighting chance for survival if we can deepen these victories.[4]

Ultimately, the objects of Kennedy's previous study—the great powers—have a role to play in these new studies but they pose a fundamental problem in their "uncertain and often fleeting ability ... to work together."[5]

Significance

Having apparently failed adequately to predict the imminent downfall of the Soviet Union, *Rise and Fall* may seem like a book of its time. Perhaps because Kennedy has since moved on to write about transnational issues, however, this earlier work retains a timeless relevance. While Kennedy wrote the final chapters of *Rise and Fall* as an addendum to the earlier chapters, it is this section of the work, with its discussion of the possibility of American decline, that people remember as most significant.

Although, as the British journalist John Crace* wrote, "Kennedy's new book, *The Rise and Fall of the Great Powers*, had touched a raw nerve, " that had not been Kennedy's intention; as he told an interviewer: "It was actually a study of more than 500 years of global empires ... but I don't think many people read more than the final chapter on the US and the USSR."[6]

The influential British financial periodical *The Economist** notes that Kennedy's thesis "looked premature"[7] because the work came out before the end of the Cold War.* But by the turn of the millennium, with the United States' commitments in Iraq* and Afghanistan, * and a financial crisis in the early 2000s, "the picture starts to look rather like the one that led Professor Kennedy to make his premature judgment."[8]

Ultimately, Kennedy's book came to symbolize Americans' anxiety that their nation may, like great powers before it, fall into decline. Kennedy continues to wield national influence on this subject. Decades after the publication of his book, policymakers still consult him as an authority on American decline.

---

1. Paul Kennedy, *The Rise and Fall of British Naval Mastery* (London: Allen Lane, 1976), 140.

2. Paul Kennedy, *The Rise of the Anglo-German Antagonism: 1860–1914* (London: George Allen & Unwin, 1980), 464.

3. Neal Acherson, "Interview with Paul Kennedy, " *Independent,* March 28, 1993, accessed September 12, 2015, http://www.independent.co.uk/voices/interview-prepare-to-meet-thy-future-big-books-about-the-21st-century-are-supposed-to-make-your-flesh-creep-but-paul-kennedy-argues-that-the-end-of-the-world-is-not-quite-nigh-1500508.html.

4. John Ikenberry, "Review of *Parliament of Man, " Foreign Affairs* 85, no. 6 (2006): 156.

5. Ikenberry, "Review, " 156.

6. John Crace, "Paul Kennedy: Neocons' Worst Nightmare, " *Guardian*, February 5, 2008, accessed September 3, 2015, http://www.theguardian.com/education/2008/feb/05/academicexperts. highereducationprofile.

7. John Ikenberry, "Imperial Overstretch?" *The Economist*, June 27, 2002, accessed September 12, 2015, http://www.economist.com/node/1188741.

8. Ikenberry, "Imperial Overstretch?"

SECTION 3
IMPACT

THE FIRST RESPONSES

KEY POINTS

- Critics accused Kennedy of making his theory too broad, and too full of assumptions that sidelined either domestic priorities or diplomatic maneuvering.
- Kennedy responded by suggesting that his critics oversimplified his theory and focused too much on the short term.
- The Cold War* ended four years after the publication of *Rise and Fall*. After that, critics fell into two camps: those who believed the United States would be the sole world power, and those who believed that international polarity* would shift from one power (unipolarity) to many powers (multipolarity).*

Criticism

Paul Kennedy's *The Rise and Fall of the Great Powers* quickly became a source of discussion—both critical and supportive. The American military strategist Edward Luttwak* suggests that Kennedy did not write the book as a "historian, " but as a "publicist"[1] who set out with a theory in mind. Rather than trying to test this theory against other theories, Kennedy asserts (says Luttwak) that societies experience different rates of growth because they "just do." Luttwak notes, "he does not, for example, argue that comparable societies have different rates of growth because their societal priorities are different."[2]

The American political strategist Joseph Nye, Jr.* argued that, especially in the post-Cold War era, we need to reconceptualize power. Nye coined the phrase "soft power, " which contrasts "to the hard command power usually associated with tangible resources like military and economic strength." Soft power convinces rather than compels.[3] Examples of soft power include technology, popular culture, and leadership in international institutions.When the world listens to American pop music, the argument goes, the United States gains a kind of cultural legitimacy that rewards Americans with both money and influence. How does having globally important pop culture lead to power? "A country that stands astride popular channels of communication, " Nye argues, "has more opportunities to get its messages across and to affect the preferences of others."[4] Nye's criticisms pointed out that Kennedy might have overlooked some dimensions of power relevant in the present day.

The next thread of criticism focused on the link between power and economic prosperity. In a colorfully titled essay "Beware of Historians Bearing False Analogies, " one American political theorist noted that "relative reduction in military outlays does not automatically translate into a higher growth rate."[5] The American professor of international affairs Charles Kupchan* takes this argument further, citing the decline of the British Empire* in the early twentieth century; Britain's economic predominance was dropping "not because of excessive military expenditure" (in fact, military expenses were decreasing) but "because of rapid economic growth in other countries and the failure of British industry to adapt to technological change."[6] In the twentieth century, newly industrializing states with regional rivals, such as South Korea,* enjoy "high rates of growth while maintaining relatively high levels of military spending."[7] Kupchan believes military spending can damage the economy, but it can also help the economy—new technologies often emerge from military research, for example. He concludes that the relationship Kennedy suggests is ill defined, and may merely be one of many possible relationships.

> "Kennedy's predictions have not fared well over the past decade and more. Russia did indeed continue to decline, but not for the reasons Kennedy argued. Russia kept sinking even after it shed the burdens of the Soviet empire and military interventions in Afghanistan and elsewhere. The other powers that Kennedy predicted would decline did not decline at all. The United States experienced a spectacular rebirth, not only 'winning' the Cold War but becoming once again the dominant economic power in the world."
>
> —— Henry Nau, "Why *The Rise and Fall of the Great Powers* Was Wrong"

Responses

Kennedy suggests that Luttwak has oversimplified his theory. Yes, great powers became overextended and exhausted, and fell but this remains "an accompanying cause, not the central factor" of why states enjoy varying levels of power and influence.[8] Kennedy presents a more nuanced version of this argument. Great powers (including the United States) show "a very significant correlation *over the longer term* between productive and revenue-raising capacities on the one hand and military strength on the other."[9]

More important to the concept of overreach, Kennedy identifies a lag time between a power's economic decline and its military decline. When a state faces decline, strategic commitments will naturally take precedence over economic capacity.This hastens the fall.[10] Essentially, the two forces interact mutually: economic decline precedes overreach, overreach makes economic recovery more difficult.Toward the end of the Cold War, even if American military spending had shrunk *in absolute terms*, it still remained higher relative to the United States' current economic prosperity, which can be problematic—a counter-argument that also applies to Kupchan.

Kupchan criticized Kennedy for over-generalizing and for imagining too simplistic a relationship between economic and military factors. Imperial overreach and economic decline, Kennedy argued, frequently go hand in hand; it was not that military spending is directly correlated to economic decline.

Conflict and Consensus

The Cold War ended just four years after *Rise and Fall* was published. It is generally agreed that the world then entered a "unipolar" phase, meaning that the United States was the only major world power. This position, first outlined by American political commentator Charles Krauthammer, * holds that "the immediate post-Cold War world is not multipolar ... The center of world power is an unchallenged superpower, the United States, attended by its Western allies."[11] Essentially, it appeared to Krauthammer and others that, far from declining due to imperial overreach, the United States would not only continue to be *a* great power, it would be the *only* great power, as no states could challenge its position.There were, roughly, two positions: either American power would decline or the country would remain alone as a superpower.

The American political scientist Henry Nau* took issue with Kennedy's predictions about American decline after the end of the Cold War. In his provocatively titled essay "Why *The Rise and Fall of the Great Powers* Was Wrong, " Nau argued that Kennedy had ignored the impact of identity and domestic politics. For Nau, history is not the story of great powers rising and falling. In his view, "democratic powers succeed best in creating wealth and power, " reducing the need for military competition and creating greater peace (and productivity) among all states.[12] Essentially, Nau suggested that the United States' democratic, capitalist* system, with elections and private wealth, made it less prone to decline than previous great powers.The United States' political and economic systems could break the pattern of decline Kennedy found inevitable. Kennedy did not respond directly to Nau's argument, but rather suggested that "his predictions might be more appropriately assessed after another decade or so"—that is, around 2010.[13]

1. Paul Kennedy and Edward Luttwak, "*The Rise and Fall of the Great Powers*: An Exchange, " *American Scholar* 59, no. 2 (1990): 287.

2. Kennedy and Luttwak, "*The Rise and Fall of the Great Powers*, " 289.

3. Joseph Nye, Jr., "The Changing Nature of World Power, " *Political Science Quarterly* 105, issue 2 (1990): 181.

4. Joseph Nye, Jr., "Soft Power, " *Foreign Policy* no. 80 (1990): 169.

5. W. W. Rostow, "Beware of Historians Bearing False Analogies, " *Foreign Affairs* 66, no. 4 (1988): 868.

6. Charles Kupchan, "Empire, Military Power, and Economic Decline, " *International Security* 13, no. 4 (1989): 42.

7. Kupchan, "Empire, Military Power, and Economic Decline, " 45.

8. Kennedy and Luttwak, *"The Rise and Fall of the Great Powers*, " 285.

9. Kennedy and Luttwak, *"The Rise and Fall of the Great Powers*, " 285.

10. Kennedy and Luttwak, *"The Rise and Fall of the Great Powers*, " 285.

11. Charles Krauthammer, "The Unipolar Moment, " *Foreign Affairs* 70, no. 1 (1990/91): 23.

12. Henry Nau, "Why *The Rise and Fall of the Great Powers* Was Wrong, " *Review of International Studies* 27, no. 4 (2001): 592.

13. Nau, "Why *The Rise and Fall of the Great Powers* Was Wrong, " 580.

THE EVOLVING DEBATE

KEY POINTS

* The question of the United States' decline remains open, even after the terrorist attacks of September 11, 2001 ("9/11")* and the problems arising from the "War on Terror"* (the United States' military operations in the Middle East and Africa against terrorist organizations).

* The term "big history"* refers to the study of history that analyzes one major concept or category over a long time period.

* The Indian American writer Fareed Zakaria* may be the most important theorist of American decline today; for him, while the world is becoming "post-American, " the United States' prestige might be preserved if the nation increased its toleration of others.

Uses And Problems

After Paul Kennedy published *The Rise and Fall of the Great Powers* in 1987, the United States enjoyed seemingly unchallenged power throughout the 1990s, and his "decline" thesis fell out of fashion in the early years of the twenty-first century. In a remarkable about-face, Kennedy wrote in a 2002 *Financial Times** article that the United States has maintained its unipolar* hegemony*—that is, its dominance. He cautioned, however, that this role "very much rests upon a decade of impressive economic growth, " and that loss of this growth might cause "the threat of overreach [to] return" as the country's military commitments increased after the terrorist attacks on US soil committed on September 11, 2001—the atrocities known as 9/11.[1]

In 2003, Kennedy, the American political strategist Joseph Nye, Jr., * and the political consultant Richard Perle* participated in a symposium called "The Reluctant Empire." The panel primarily focused on how the United States should secure itself in a post-9/11 world, especially in light of the war in Iraq.* Recapitulating some of his economic argument, Kennedy suggested that a protracted war in Iraq would affect domestic prosperity but he spent most of his time talking about the consequences the war would have for the United States' "soft power."* Beyond the cost in civilian lives, he argued, the war would also reduce the influence of international organizations, because the US began the war unilaterally and without the authorization of the United Nations.*[2]

Kennedy did not confine his remarks here to the relationship between economics and strategy, as his discussion of the "soft power" consequences of the Iraq War shows. Ultimately, though, Kennedy believes the United States has allowed its security commitments to create a kind of "empire, " since it wields "a global influence that is disproportionate to a country that has less than 5 percent of the world's population."[3]

After 9/11 ratcheted up the United States' quasi-imperial commitments abroad, the financial crisis* of 2007–8 diminished economic resources at home—and Kennedy reaffirmed his belief in American decline once again. In an article for the US financial periodical the *Wall Street Journal*, * he argued, "The data so far suggest the economies of China and India are growing (not as fast as in the past but still growing), while America's economy shrinks in absolute terms." Because of that, the United States should not expect its share of total world production to remain at the height it reached in previous years.[4] He concludes that this situation heralds a "global tectonic power shift" westward across the Pacific, from America to Asia. It remains up to the government of the United States to handle that shift.

> "The most significant political phenomenon of our new century is going to be the relative rise of Asia, perhaps China especially, and its natural concomitant, the relative decline of the west as a whole and more particularly of both of its two greatest components, Europe and the US."
> —— Paul Kennedy, *Rise and Fall of the Great Powers*

Schools of Thought

Rise and Fall may be considered a work of scholarship relevant to the disciplines of history and of political science. For Kennedy, it is a work of "big history, "* which he defines as "single-volume books whose authors took hold of a vast topic and then wrestled it to the ground, comprehended it, and explained it to readers."[5] In effect, "big history" represents a theorized approach to history that aims to explain some large category of event. In Kennedy's case, this category could be the relative strength of great powers. In the case of the Scottish historian Niall Ferguson, * another scholar in this genre and a similarly popular writer, the category would be the advent of global Western dominance—and the threat other states pose to that continued dominance. Ferguson suggests that in 1500 the notion that Western Europe would come to dominate the world "would have come to seem wildly fanciful." He asks "what was it about the civilization of Western Europe after the fifteenth century that allowed it to trump the outwardly superior empires of the Orient?"[6] Ferguson investigates the ascendancy of the West so "we can hope to estimate … the imminence of our decline and fall."[7]

In Current Scholarship

Fareed Zakaria, perhaps the most important "declinist"* working today (that is, a proponent of the belief that the power and influence of the United States is waning), may be best known for his 2009 book *The Post-American World.* He notes that "for the roughly two decades since 1989, the power of the United States has defined the international order, " meaning the nation remained the only relevant political player. This stemmed from a complex mix of factors— economic, military, and the mere fact of being the only great power standing after the Cold War.*

Politics today has moved on though.[8] If the world continues to be defined by the United States' remaining—and waning— strength, "several other important great powers" such as China, Russia, or the European Union* must be factored into any analysis. Zakaria sees "greater assertiveness and activity from all actors."[9] Essentially, Zakaria argues, as US economic and military power declines relative to others, no other nation is attempting to supplant the United States. The truth is that the rising powers simply care about one another more. Zakaria sees the strength of the United

States in its openness, and suggests that to keep the world from becoming too "post-American, " the country must bolster its commitment to openness and tolerance.[10] In Zakaria's estimation, openness encourages the goodwill of others, harnesses the best abilities of the country's population, and attracts talent from abroad.

1. Paul Kennedy, "The Eagle Has Landed, " *Financial Times*, February 1, 2002.
2. Paul Kennedy et al., "The Reluctant Empire: In a Time of Great Consequence, " *Brown Journal of World Affairs* 10, no. 1 (2003): 16.
3. Kennedy et al., "The Reluctant Empire, " 16.
4. Paul Kennedy, "American Power is on the Wane, " *Wall Street Journal,* January 1, 2009, accessed September 14, 2015, http://www.wsj.com/articles/SB123189377673479433.
5. Paul Kennedy, "The Distant Horizon: What Can 'Big History' Tell Us About America's Future?" *Foreign Affairs* 87, no. 3 (2008) : 126–7.
6. Niall Ferguson, *Civilization: The West and the Rest* (London: Allen Lane, 2010), 8.
7. Ferguson, *Civilization*, 18.
8. Fareed Zakaria, *The Post-American World* (New York: W.W. Norton and Company, 2008), 42.
9. Zakaria, *The Post-American World*, 43.
10. Zakaria, *The Post-American World*, 257.

MODULE 11
IMPACT AND INFLUENCE TODAY

KEY POINTS

* *Rise and Fall* remains best known for raising important questions about American decline, and how the United States should manage its own loss of hegemony* to China.
* Some argue that the United States should fight its decline and accept its role as a global leader, as leadership delivers significant benefits (in terms of agenda-setting, soft power, * and economic returns) relative to its cost.
* Opponents argue that the benefits of global engagement do not outweigh the costs. They feel that the United States ought to reconsider and adopt a more sustainable role in international affairs.

Position

Paul Kennedy wrote *The Rise and Fall of the Great Powers* as a work of history, spanning the period from 1500 to the latter half of the twentieth century. For Americans concerned with national decline, it remains most relevant as a work of political science. Still, many international relations scholars today have become concerned more with the issue of hegemony than with pure power, and Kennedy's way of examining the international system seems less applicable.

Through his discussion of "world hegemony, " the Italian political economist Giovanni Arrighi* provides an alternative to the notion of European "great power" competition; for him, it is "the power of a state to exercise functions of leadership and governance over a system of sovereign states."[1] For theorists of international history like Arrighi, the concept of "hegemony" became more interesting than that of "great power, " as its roots lie in the capacity both to define and rule the international system. These theorists would find it meaningless to assume that great powers were a feature of Europe alone. For them, Europeans exercise hegemonic control over the rest of the world, defining the world system in their own image.

Rise and Fall does not play a defining role in the debate about the ways in which the United States should conduct itself. Instead, as the most important statement of the thesis that the United States is in decline, it raises questions "about the structural, fiscal and economic weaknesses in America that, over time, could nibble away at the foundations of US power."[2] The 1990s delivered a period of unprecedented growth and international esteem, causing some to dismiss predictions of decline. But according to the American scholar Christopher Layne, * in the wake of the financial crisis* of 2007–8, the theory gained new traction.[3] A landmark study by the Brookings Institution*—an influential body that aims to influence US foreign policy—attributes the source of "relative decline" to the rise of China. China's regional power has increased, in no small part facilitated by explosive economic growth. And this growth, in turn, has fueled an expansion of China's military capability.[4] The Brookings report defines the relationship between China and the United States as "strategic distrust"—a perception that "the other side will seek to achieve its key long term goals at concerted cost to your own side's core prospects and interests."[5]

> *"In modern history, there have been two liberal international orders: **Pax Britannica** and **Pax Americana**. In building their respective international structures, Britain and the United States wielded their power to advance their own economic and geopolitical interests. But they also bestowed important benefits— public goods—on the international system as a whole."*
>
> —— Christopher Layne, "The End of the Pax Americana"

Interaction

Kennedy said that dominant countries face dilemmas as they decline—specifically a reduction in economic strength and growing strategic commitments abroad. To preserve prestige in the face of these dilemmas, is it better to allocate more funds to the military, or pull back?[6] In a 2013 article called "Lean Forward," the American scholars Stephen Brooks, * John Ikenberry* and William Wohlforth* wrote, "Washington might be tempted to ... pull back from the world. The rise of China is chipping away at the United States' preponderance of power [and] a budget crisis has put defense spending on the chopping block."[7] In light of this, they endorsed the notion of spending more on international commitments; as they explained it, the United States might be tempted to avoid "imperial overreach" by pulling back from its strategic commitments, and redress a growing rift between its power resources and economic resources. But as costly as the US's global commitments may be, they play a more central role in the nation's prosperity than we might imagine; in the authors' words, "military dominance undergirds its economic leadership."[8]

The global dominance of the United States allows the country to serve the common good in many important ways. The US Navy secures sea lanes.The US dollar serves as the world's reserve currency.* And the US offers its allies economic leverage in their military expenditures. Allies can maintain smaller defense budgets because the US has guaranteed their security both bilaterally and under the NATO* pact.[9] The US enjoys disproportionate gains from these expensive outlays because they help "prevent the outbreak of conflict in the world's most important regions, keep the global economy humming, and make international cooperation easier" for everyone, and allow the US to shape what the world looks like.[10]

The Continuing Debate

The American political scientist Barry Posen* wrote a companion piece to "Lean Forward, " entitled "Pull Back." Posen agrees with Kennedy that the United States should have fewer global entanglements. In *Rise and Fall*, Kennedy had written, "The task facing American statesmen over the next decades is to recognize that broad trends are under way, and that there is a need to 'manage' affairs so that the *relative* erosion of the United States' position takes place slowly and smoothly."[11]

Posen argues that the US ought to manage its decline by slowly reducing the world's dependence on its generosity. For example, taking on the defense burdens of many European and Asian allies and entangling itself in conflicts abroad in order to further its international agenda brings with it consequences: it "makes enemies almost as fast as it slays them, discourages allies from paying for their own defense, and convinces powerful states to band together and oppose Washington's plans, further raising the costs of carrying out its foreign policy."[12]

Posen sees the United States as trying singlehandedly to maintain global security. While the US undertakes drawn-out occupations of failed states and maintains security agreements with China's Taiwan, Japan, and Europe, other states and region fail to shoulder the burden of global security. Posen argues for a "nimble" grand strategy, where states combat terrorism with "carefully applied force, rather than through wholesale nation-building efforts such as that in Afghanistan."[13] Essentially, "if the US debt keeps growing and power continues to shift to other countries, some future economic or political crisis could force Washington to switch course abruptly."[14] If the United States were to pull back rapidly, it would create a vacuum for other powers such as China to assume its leadership role.

---

1. Giovanni Arrighi, *The Long Twentieth Century: Money, Power, and the Origins of Our Times* (London: Verso, 2002), 27.

2. Christopher Layne, "The End of the Pax Americana: How Western Decline Became Inevitable," *The Atlantic,* April 2012, accessed September 14, 2015, http://www.theatlantic.com/international/archive/2012/04/the-end-of-pax-americana-how-western-decline-became-inevitable/256388/.

3. Layne, "The End of the Pax Americana."

4. Kenneth Lieberthal and Wang Jisi, *Addressing US–China Strategic Distrust* (Washington, DC: Brookings Institution, 2012), 2–3.

5. Lieberthal and Jisi, *Addressing US–China Strategic Distrust,* 5.

6. Paul Kennedy, *The Rise and Fall of the Great Powers* (New York: Vintage Books, 1989), 533.

7. Stephen Brooks et al., "Lean Forward: In Defense of American Engagement, " *Foreign Affairs* 92,

no. 1 (2013): 130.

8. Brooks et al., "Lean Forward, " 138.

9. Brooks et al., "Lean Forward, " 138.

10. Brooks et al., "Lean Forward, " 139.

11. Kennedy, *Rise and Fall*, 534.

12. Barry Posen, "Pull Back: The Case for a Less Activist Foreign Policy, " *Foreign Affairs* 92, no. 1 (2013): 117.

13. Posen, "Pull Back, " 122.

14. Posen, "Pull Back, " 128.

MODULE 12
WHERE NEXT?

KEY POINTS

* Kennedy has recently argued that China is rising relative to the United States in both economic and military terms.

* The American lawyer and scholar Philip Bobbitt* argued that war has changed in the twenty-first century. In the past, only states had the capacity to create mass violence. Today, technology has made it possible for smaller, less well-funded groups to wreak havoc.

* While *Rise and Fall* was important as a work of history, it is primarily remembered by and debated within the field of political science for its prediction that the United States would experience a decline following the Cold War.*

Potential

While *The Rise and Fall of the Great Powers* may be important as a work of international history, Paul Kennedy remains an active participant in the debate over how the United States will accommodate (or resist) the decline predicted in the book's final chapters. Kennedy points out that "Asia is growing at a significantly faster pace than the mature economies of the US and Europe, " especially in terms of the balance of capital.[1] He notes that "surplus bank savings have usually accompanied the alterations in the military-political balances of power ... from the Lombard cities to Antwerp and Amsterdam; from there to London; from London ... to New York; and from New York ... to where? Shanghai?" Simply put, Asia has increasingly become wealthier and financially more important than the West.

The military balance has also shifted, especially as it relates to sea power (which includes aircraft carriers). Kennedy thinks American strategists must be asking, "Why is Beijing spending so much on defense?" Even if China's defense budget remains lower in absolute terms, is it growing relatively? "Why this heavy investment into cyber-warfare?; into military satellites?; into commercial espionage? What about those medium-range sea-skimming missiles that fly below the radar screens of US warships, and those ultra-long-range rockets that can cross the wide Pacific?"[2] If China's naval capabilities (and therefore, its ability to project power worldwide) are growing *relative* to the United States, is American domination of the Pacific Ocean not shrinking? The Pacific encompasses half the world. In *Rise and Fall*, Kennedy argues that power can be measured both financially and militarily. It seems that China's power is growing and the United States' shrinking; we may be witnessing the relative decline of a great power.

> "We must urgently develop legal and strategic parameters for state action in the Wars against Terror. Ultimately this will be a matter of drawing the links between successfully warring on terror and evolving legal concepts of sovereignty and its relationship to lawful, legitimate governance."
>
> — Philip Bobbitt, *Terror and Consent*

Future Directions

One prominent successor to Kennedy's project of discussing the

United States' place in the world is Philip Bobbitt. His books *The Shield of Achilles:War, Peace, and the Course of History* (2002) and *Terror and Consent:The Wars for the Twenty-first Century* (2008) both present a picture of history in which technological change, constitutional change, and economic change work together. Bobbitt notes that the "objective" of the wide-ranging "War on Terror"* being fought by the United States, largely in the Middle East and Africa, "is not the conquest of territory or the silencing of any particular ideology"—the kind of war Paul Kennedy might recognize. Instead, Bobbitt says it is "to secure the environment necessary for states of consent and to make it impossible for our enemies to impose or induce states of terror."[3]

Bobbitt identifies what he calls "states of consent"—Western states that depend on the consent of citizens for their legitimacy and see their primary job as protecting those civilians. The growth of technology and connectedness has enabled this protection to enter a new realm. Where is the threat? Bobbitt's assessment of the United States' strength in the face of this new kind of enemy stands in stark contrast to Kennedy's in *Rise and Fall*.The US has the world's largest economy. It supports "a large army equipped with infinitely superior weaponry and communications." But "the harm that can be done to the American nation is growing more quickly (as technology disperses and becomes cheaper) than its lead is increasing."[4]

In other words, Bobbitt believes technology has altered the dynamics Kennedy analyzed in the late twentieth century. The capacity to do large-scale violence used to be the exclusive province of states. And in part, the robustness of the economy defined this capacity; such violence required too many resources for entities other than nations to consider it.Today, in Bobbitt's view, military might and the economy have become less important than cohesiveness among states and forward planning in the face of terror. In effect, states will survive if they can remain networked with one another, and anticipate threats.

Summary

Paul Kennedy's *The Rise and Fall of the Great Powers* is first and foremost a work of history. Kennedy analyzes the powers that have really mattered in the world since 1500 and determines the factors that enabled these powers to rise to that level of prominence. He also warns of forces that might cause their prominence to fall. Despite the thorough historical analysis it contains, scholars remember *Rise and Fall* as a work of political science. Its final chapters, added almost as an afterthought, captured the fears of the time: that the United States might be a great power due to fall.

Kennedy argues that strategy and economics are intimately bound. A state rises to prominence because it enjoys relative growth and superior productive capacity. Kennedy measures this in industrial and agricultural production, the very basics of prosperity, rather than simple resource endowment. Economic prosperity enables the state to create a fighting force that can prevail in any battle and a "great power" is born. When the growing state overcommits—often, paradoxically, to protect material wealth—"imperial overreach" sets in. States will find themselves like an old man carrying a heavy burden up a hill: other powers with relatively more dynamic economies, and fewer foreign commitments soaking up resources from those economies, will catch up and outpace those slowing down.

This is not only a powerful (if very simple) paradigm* to understand history, it also served as a powerful warning to the United States that it must not move to create an "empire" of its own at the end of the Cold War. Otherwise, it would tread the well-worn path to decline, as have the other great powers in Kennedy's work.

---

1. Paul Kennedy, "Asia's Rise: Rise and Fall, " *The World Today* 66, no. 8/9 (2010): 7.
2. Kennedy, "Asia's Rise: Rise and Fall, " 7.
3. Philip Bobbitt, *Terror and Consent: The Wars for the Twenty-first Century* (London: Penguin, 2009), 3.
4. Bobbitt, *Terror and Consent*, 537.

GLOSSARY OF TERMS

1. **Aberystwyth University:** a research University in Wales, in the United Kingdom.

2. **Afghanistan War:** a military conflict starting in 2001 in which a United States-led NATO coalition fought al-Qaeda and the Taliban.

3. **Anarchy:** a condition in which there is no administrative or governing authority to enforce rules.

4. **Annales school:** a French school of historical thought that emphasizes the long-term influences on day-to-day living, through interdisciplinary methods (methods that draw on the aims and methods of different academic disciplines, in this case geography, economics, and sociology).This contrasted with the more traditional way of studying history, which presented dramatic events in sequence.

5. **Außenpolitik:** a German term referring to "the politics of outside." It suggests that foreign policy is the most important activity pursued by states.

6. **Big history:** a theorized approach to history that aims to explain a large category or concept.The term is also used to describe the recently emerging study of the entire history of the universe from its beginnings in the big bang to the present.

7. **Bipolar:** an international order characterized by two opposing state powers.

8. **British Empire (sixteenth to twentieth centuries):** the areas of the world under direct control by Britain.After World War I, it comprised up to 25 percent of the world's land and 20 percent of its population.While the empire fell into serious decline in the aftermath of World War II, scholars generally mark its end as the return of Hong Kong to China in 1997.

9. **Brookings Institution:** an American think tank, considered the world's most influential, that aims to affect American foreign policy. In general, it supports a more open and interconnected international system.

10. **Capitalism:** an economic system that emphasizes private property rights and the pursuit of profit from privately owned industry.

11. **Cold War (1947–91):** a period of tension between the United States and the

Soviet Union. While the two countries never engaged in direct military conflict, they were involved in covert and proxy wars and espionage against one another.

12. **Communism:** a political ideology that advocates state ownership of the means of production, the collectivization of labor, and the abolition of social class. It was the ideology of the Soviet Union (1917–89) and stood in contrast to free-market capitalism during the Cold War.

13. **Cuban Missile Crisis (1962):** the closest the United States and Soviet Union came to a nuclear exchange. It arose over a dispute between the US and USSR about deployment of Soviet missiles in Cuba.

14. **Declinism:** a belief that one's country or institution faces irreversible worsening in its overall position in the world.

15. **Dynasty:** a family line of heads of states.

16. **The Economist:** an English-language magazine, published in London since 1843, that analyzes economic and political issues at a relatively sophisticated level. Its editorial stance is "classical liberalism, " which entails free enterprise and personal liberty.

17. **European Union:** founded in 1993 as a set of supranational (meaning above governments) and intergovernmental (meaning between governments) institutions. The EU administers and coordinates policy among 28 European states.

18. **Falklands War (1982):** a conflict between Argentina and the United Kingdom over the territory of the Falkland Islands in the South Atlantic. The conflict claimed nearly 1,000 lives and resulted in a British victory.

19. **Financial crisis (2007–2008):** a major economic depression, the worst since the 1930s. Unemployment increased around the world, while economic production decreased.

20. **Financial Times:** an English-language newspaper, published in London beginning in 1888, which focuses on business and economics.

21. **Foreign Affairs:** a professional and academic journal founded in 1921.

Published by the Council on Foreign Relations in NewYork, it offers an American focus on international politics.

22. **Gross National Product (GNP):** the market value of all goods and services produced in one year by the residents of a country.

23. **Habsburg Dynasty (1438–1918):** a European family that, at its most powerful, ruled portions of southern Italy, Spain, Austria, the German city states, Hungary, and other areas in Central and Western Europe. It was known for using marriage rather than conquest to increase its political influence.

24. **Hegemony:** a concept relating to the dominance of a group by one individual— the "hegemon" is notable not only for compelling others to do or not do a thing, but for actually establishing the "rules of the game."

25. **Hindenburg Programme (1916):** the policy Germany adopted to vastly increase its military production in World War I. Ultimately, the plan (which diverted all German economic efforts to "war relevant" industries) led to disaster and starvation, and Germany's downfall.

26. **Holy Roman Empire:** a network of territories in Europe that endured from the ninth century until it was dissolved in 1806.The empire encompassed large parts of Austria, the Netherlands, Naples, and other territories around Europe.

27. **International relations:** the study of the relationships between states in a global system, primarily linked to foreign policy. It includes the study of supranational organizations such as the World Bank and other non-government organizations (NGOs).

28. **Iraq War (2003–11):** an armed conflict initially between Iraq and the United States, and then between a protracted insurgency and the United States.The United States and its allies believed that Saddam Hussein, the then-leader of Iraq, had secretly built a stockpile of nuclear weapons.

29. **Korean War (1950–53):** a war between North and South Korea, which arose from the division of Korea after World War II, and the tensions of the Cold War. A United Nations force led by the United States fought for the South; China

fought for the North, with the help of the Soviet Union.

30. **Longue durée:** a French phrase meaning "long term." It refers, in the context of history, to the approach taken by the historians of the *Annales* school, who were concerned with historical changes (often social changes) over the long term.

31. **Ming Dynasty (1368–1644):** a Chinese imperial dynasty. Ming rulers led a campaign to centralize Chinese institutions and created a standing army.They were also known for (partly) overseeing the building of grand structures such as the Great Wall.

32. **Mongol Empire (1206–1368):** the lands in Eurasia conquered by Mongolian warlord Temujin—better known as Genghis Khan—and his successors.At its peak it encompassed 1.27 million square miles from southeast Asia to eastern Europe.

33. **Multipolar:** an international order characterized by the equal importance of several state powers.

34. **NATO:** North Atlantic Treaty Organization, a military alliance between governments whose members guarantee to defend one another in the face of external attack.The alliance is led by the United States and has 28 members including all the major European powers. It derives from the North Atlantic Treaty, signed in the aftermath of World War II in 1949 by the US, France, Britain, Canada, and others.

35. **Newcastle University:** a public research university in Newcastle, founded in 1963.

36. **9/11:** a term referring to four coordinated terror attacks launched against the United States by the Islamic extremist group al-Qaeda on September 11, 2001. Four passenger airplanes were flown into various targets around the country, including the twin towers of the World Trade Center in NewYork City, and the Pentagon in Washington, DC.

37. **Paradigm:** a worldview that underpins the theories of a particular subject. For instance, the idea that states conflict, rather than cooperate, remains central to the

paradigm of international relations realism.

38. **Pax Americana:** a Latin phrase meaning "American Peace." It refers to the long period of global stability (between great powers, if not domestically) in the second half of the twentieth century. But numerous proxy wars between the great powers, regimes throughout the global south sustained by authoritarian violence, and civil wars cast doubt on the overall peacefulness of the time.

39. **Pax Britannica:** a period of relative stability (at least between Western powers) experienced while Britain was at the height of its global power in the nineteenth century.

40. **Polarity:** the distribution of power within the international system—a bipolar system has power concentrated in two states, while a multipolar system has power concentrated in multiple states.

41. **Reagan doctrine:** a foreign policy strategy followed during the presidency of Ronald Reagan with the intention of diminishing the influence or power of the Soviet Union; anti-communist paramilitary forces were funded with the intention of destabilizing communist nations, and large sums of money were spent on arms provision.

42. **Reserve currency:** a stock of money held by governments so they may conduct international transactions.The US dollar is currently the most important currency, as it is the currency in which trades are agreed between states that do not use the US dollar as their native currency.

43. **Roman Empire (27 B.C.E.–385 C.E.):** the territorial holdings of the Roman state.The Roman Republic became the Empire when Julius Caesar declared himself dictator.At its height, it encompassed the entire Mediterranean, and significant portions of the Near East. In 385 c.e. it split into a western half, which fell to northern invasion in 476, and an eastern half, which became the Byzantine Empire, and fell to the Ottomans in 1453.

44. **St. Antony's College:** a postgraduate-only college at the University of Oxford, founded in 1950. It specializes in "area studies, " meaning close study of a given geographic area, such as East Asia or Africa.

45. **Socialism:** a political system in which the means of production (the tools and resources required by business and industry) are held in common ownership.

46. **Soft power:** a concept developed by American political thinker Joseph Nye, Jr., the phrase refers to a form of cultural imperialism, leadership imposed through the "soft power" of US preeminence in technology, culture, or international governance through organizations such as the United Nations rather than the "hard power" associated with economic or military force.

47. **South Korea:** the southern half of the Korean peninsula in East Asia, South Korea has a highly advanced economy.Along with Hong Kong of China, Singapore and Taiwan of China (the "Asian Tigers"), it experienced rapid economic growth from the 1960s onward.

48. **Soviet Union/Union of Soviet Socialist Republics (USSR):** a super-state encompassing communist countries in Europe and Central Asia, with its capital in Moscow. Founded in 1922, it dissolved with the end of the Cold War in 1991.

49. **Sphere of influence:** a concept in politics, most significant during the Cold War.A state's "sphere of influence" represents an area in which they wield special authority, even over other states.

50. **Superpower:** a term most commonly used with reference to the United States and the Soviet Union in the Cold War, because these nations held more power than any other nation in history.

51. **Totalitarian:** refers to a system of government in which obedience to the state remains the most important aspect of daily life.

52. **United Nations:** an intergovernmental organization representing (nearly) every state in the world. It is the main organization administering international health, development, security, and similar programs.

53. **University of Oxford:** a collegiate research-focused university in Oxford, in the United Kingdom. It is the oldest university in the English-speaking world. Teaching in Oxford began—it is believed—in the eleventh century, though the first of its colleges was founded in the thirteenth century; different colleges

dispute this honor.

54. **Vietnam War:** a two-decade-long military conflict between communist forces, led by North Vietnam, and anti-communist forces, led by the United States and South Vietnam. Starting in 1955 and finishing in 1975 after American troops withdrew from Vietnamese territory, it was the longest proxy war fought by the United States during the Cold War.

55. **Wall Street Journal:** an English-language newspaper, published in NewYork since 1889, that focuses on business issues and economics.

56. **War on Terror:** the term commonly applied to American-led actions throughout the Middle East against non-state "terrorist" actors, including al-Qaeda.The effort includes the drone campaign in Pakistan, the occupation of Afghanistan, and other covert and overt operations.

57. **Warsaw Pact (1955–91):** a military alliance between the eight communist states in Eastern Europe that provided security guarantees to its members.The pact dissolved as the Cold War ended.

58. **Weltpolitik:** a German term meaning "world policy, " and referring to a late-nineteenth-century German governmental policy that aimed to build up German military power while fostering an intense national pride and using tough diplomacy to establish Germany as a "great power."

59. **World systems analysis:** a method for analyzing global history that sees the "world system" of interconnecting capital and labor and other forces as the principal actor in historical change rather than "nation-states."

60. **World War I:** an international conflict from 1914 to 1918 centered in Europe and involving the major economic world powers of the day. The industrial advancements in military technology as well as the scale of the conflict resulted in vast military and civilian casualties. Some scholars see World War II as a continuation of World War I, because of unresolved tensions.

61. **World War II:** a global conflict from 1939 to 1945 that involved the world's great powers and numerous other countries around the globe. Fought between the Allies (the United States, Britain, France, the Soviet Union, and others) and

the Axis powers (Germany, Italy, Japan, and others), it was seen as a major moral struggle between freedom and tyranny and included events like the Holocaust.

62. **Yale University:** an Ivy League university in the United States. Founded in 1701, it is the third oldest university in that country.

PEOPLE MENTIONED IN THE TEXT

1. **Giovanni Arrighi (1937–2009)** was an Italian political economist and historian. His work examined the evolution of international capitalism and its attendant ideas since 1400. A political activist as well as an academic, he was jailed in 1966 while teaching in Rhodesia (now Zimbabwe).

2. **Otto von Bismarck (1815–98)** was a nineteenth-century Prussian statesman. He is considered to have been the founder of modern Germany, and was the first chancellor of a united Germany.

3. **Jeremy Black (b. 1955)** is a prolific British historian, professor of history at Exeter University in southwest England. He is a particular expert in eighteenth-century international relations and British politics.

4. **Philip Bobbitt (b. 1948)** is an American lawyer and civil servant, and an academic in the field of security studies. He has served under both Democratic and Republican governments, advising US presidents on intelligence, international law, and strategy.

5. **Fernand Braudel (1902–85)** was a French historian. Founder of the *Annales* school, he emphasized the role of large-scale, long-term socioeconomic shifts (rather than the decisions of kings) in driving history.

6. **John Brewer** is a historian at the University of California, Los Angeles, specializing in the seventeenth and eighteenth centuries.

7. **Stephen Brooks** is a professor of government at Dartmouth University. He is a public intellectual advocating a "forward"American policy."Forward" means being open to commitments abroad, and seeking an active role in solving global problems (economically, militarily, and so forth).This policy is about increasing influence rather than conserving resources.

8. **Charles V (1500–58)** was king of Spain (as Carlos I), and was also elected Holy Roman Emperor (the elected ruler of a confederation of semi-independent princely states in an area that comprises much of central Europe) in 1519. His reign was characterized by imperial expansion in the New World, and war against the French in Europe.

9. **Christopher Columbus (1451–1506)** was an Italian explorer. Though he was

looking for an alternative route to India, Columbus sailed from Europe across the Atlantic to America in 1492.

10. **John Crace** is a British journalist and author who writes in the *Guardian*. He currently writes a regular sketch on events in the House of Commons in the British Parliament.

11. **Dr. Faustus** is a character in Germanic folklore, made famous in the English language in a play by the English playwright Christopher Marlowe, first performed in 1592. He famously made a bargain with the devil, trading his immortal soul for knowledge.

12. **Niall Ferguson (b. 1964)** is a Scottish historian and popular writer, who often focuses on the special role of the West and capitalism in world history. He is occasionally the subject of media controversy due to remarks on Islam or colonialism.

13. **John Lewis Gaddis (b. 1941)** is an American professor of military and naval history at Yale University. He is considered to be the most important Cold War historian. His approach (the "great man theory") has been characterized as highlighting the role played by individuals.

14. **John Andrew Gallagher (1919–80)** was a British historian of empire at the universities of Oxford and Cambridge. His (co-written) article, "The Imperialism of Free Trade, " has been called the most-cited article ever published in the discipline of history.

15. **Samuel Huntington (1927–2008)** was an American political theorist. His 1993 article "The Clash of Civilizations?" (later developed into a book) earned him fame and notoriety. It argued that in the post-Cold War era, international conflicts would be defined by cultural divisions.

16. **John Ikenberry (b. 1954)** is an American theorist of international relations at Princeton University. He is, famously, one of the architects of the US policy of "liberal internationalism."

17. **Charles Krauthammer (1950—2018)** was an American public intellectual and Pulitzer Prize-winning journalist. He advocated a tough but restrained American

foreign policy. He originated the phrase "Reagan doctrine."

18. **Charles Kupchan (b. 1958)** is an American academic, professor of international affairs at Georgetown University and a senior fellow at the Council of Foreign Relations. Kupchan focuses on the possibility of peace and change in international affairs.

19. **Christopher Layne (b. 1949)** is the chair of intelligence and national security at Texas A&M University. He is notable for critiquing the ambitions of liberal internationalists to spread American values abroad.

20. **Richard Ned Lebow (b. 1942)** is an American political scientist and professor of international political theory at King's College London. He is considered the founder of Neoclassical Realism, an approach that holds that personality and the balance of power both remain important in determining international outcomes.

21. **Sir Basil Liddell Hart (1895–1970)** was a British military theorist at the University of Oxford. He is credited with influencing the development of rapid, tank-based warfare in the aftermath of the stationary, trench-based strategy of World War I.

22. **Edward Luttwak (b. 1942)** is an American military and political theorist. He focuses on "grand" strategy, and has written about how it has manifested itself as far back as the Roman Empire.

23. **William McNeill (1917—2016)** was a Canadian American professor (emeritus) of history at the University of Chicago. He won the National Humanities Medal in the US in 2010, recognizing his contribution to history and his teaching work.

24. **Henry Nau (b. 1941)** is professor of political science and international affairs at George Washington University. He sat on the National Security Council during the Reagan administration.

25. **Joseph Nye, Jr. (b. 1937)** is an American political science professor at Harvard University. He co-wrote *Power and Interdependence* with the American academic Robert Keohane, effectively helping found neoliberalism. He is also considered to be the father of theories of "complex interdependence, " which illustrate how states will avoid conflict with other states when their interests are bound up with

each other's success.

26. **Richard Perle (b. 1941)** is an American political consultant and former member of the Senate Armed Services Committee who also served as assistant secretary of defense under President Reagan.Today a member of many think tanks, he is a prominent member of a group of neoconservatives ("neo-cons") seeking to influence US foreign policy.

27. **Philip II (1527–98):** king of Spain, who also ruled swathes of territory throughout Europe (including, briefly, England and Ireland by virtue of his marriage to Mary I of England). During his period of influence, Spain conquered territory around the world, including the Philippines (which was named after him).

28. **Barry Posen (b. 1962)** is professor of political science at the Massachusetts Institute of Technology (MIT). He is famous for his focus on the interaction between military doctrine and foreign policy.

29. **Leopold von Ranke (1795–1886)** was a German historian, and pioneered the use of rigorous sources in the study of history.Von Ranke's rigorous approach to history has been influential.

30. **Ronald Reagan (1911–2004)** was 40th president of the United States (1981–89). A member of the Republican Party, he is widely credited in the United States with having won the Cold War. He is also remembered for promoting nationalism and the global free market.

31. **J. L. Richardson** is a lecturer in government at the University of Sydney.

32. **Friedrich Schiller (1759–1805)** was a German polymath (someone with wide knowledge in many fields). He was one of the early historians of the Thirty Years' War, but is best known as a literary figure.

33. **Oswald Spengler (1880–1936)** was a German historian (among other things), most famous for postulating that civilizations are akin to organisms with lifespans.

34. **Joseph Stalin (1878–1953)** was leader of the Soviet Union as General Secretary of the Communist Party from 1922 to his death. His brutal economic policies and

political repression caused the deaths of millions, but also made the Soviet Union into a superpower. His successor, Nikita Khruschev, denounced him as a tyrant.

35. **Janice Gross Stein (b. 1943)** is a Canadian political scientist at the Munk School of Global Affairs at the University of Toronto. She writes on many topics, including diplomacy, negotiation, and intelligence.

36. **A. J. P. Taylor (1906–90)** was a British historian who wrote on nineteenth-and twentieth-century political and diplomatic history. He is the author of the classic *The Origins of the Second World War* (1961).

37. **Harry S. Truman (1884–1972)** was the 33rd president of the United States (1945–53). He presided over the beginning of the Cold War and helped pioneer the "containment" strategy (the Truman doctrine) of keeping the Soviets from gaining international influence.

38. **Immanuel Wallerstein (1930—2019)** was an American sociologist and international historian. He was famous for his theory of the "world system, " which argues that unequal economic exchange between a set of privileged "core" states (including the United States and Europe) and unprivileged "peripheral" states (such as Africa, South America, and South Asia) characterizes modern international politics.

39. **Kenneth Waltz (1924–2013)** was an American international relations professor best known for reformulating realism to make it more scientific (this is often called neorealism). Neorealism argued that states are naturally suspicious of one another and prone to secure their position by balancing power. This theory dominated international relations from the 1970s to the 1990s.

40. **William Wohlforth (b. 1959)** is professor of government at Dartmouth College. His work emphasizes security and foreign policy.

41. **Fareed Zakaria (b. 1964)** is an Indian American journalist and author. He has been managing editor of *Foreign Affairs* and *Time*, and notably wrote *The Post-American World*. He believes the United States' importance has declined, but that it is in no danger from countries that consider the United States increasingly irrelevant.

WORKS CITED

1. Acherson, Neal. "Interview with Paul Kennedy." *Independent*, March 28, 1993. Accessed September 12, 2015. http://www.independent.co.uk/voices/interview-prepare-to-meet-thy-future-big-books-about-the-21st-century-are-supposed-to-make-your-flesh-creep-but-paul-kennedy-argues-that-the-end-of-the-world-is-not-quite-nigh-1500508.html.

2. Arrighi, Giovanni. *The Long Twentieth Century: Money, Power, and the Origins of Our Times.* London: Verso, 2002.

3. Black, Jeremy. *Great Powers and the Quest for Hegemony: The World Order Since 1500.* London: Routledge, 2008.

4. Bobbitt, Philip. *The Shield of Achilles: War, Peace and Course of History.* London: Allen Lane, 2002.

5. ____.*Terror and Consent: The Wars for the Twenty-first Century.* London: Penguin, 2008.

6. Braudel, Fernand. *The Mediterranean and Mediterranean World in the Age of Philip II.* Translated by Siân Reynolds. New York: Harper & Row, 1972.

7. Brewer, John. *The Sinews of Power: War, Money, and the English State 1688–1783.* London: Century Hutchinson, 1988.

8. Brooks, Stephen, John Ikenberry, and William Wohlforth. "Lean Forward: In Defense of American Engagement." *Foreign Affairs* 92, no. 1 (2013): 130–42.

9. Chua, Amy. *Day of Empire: How Hyperpowers Rise to Global Dominance—And Why They Fall.* London: Doubleday, 2007.

10. Clark, William P. *United States National Security Decision Directive 75.* Washington, DC: 1983.

11. Crace, John. "Paul Kennedy: Neocons' Worst Nightmare." *Guardian*, February 5, 2008. Accessed September 3, 2015. http://www.theguardian.com/education/2008/feb/05/academicexperts.highereducationprofile.

12. Craig, Gordon A. "The Historian and the Study of International Relations." *American Historical Review* 88, no. 1 (1983): 1–11.

13. Epstein, Katherine. "Scholarship and the Ship of State: Rethinking the Anglo-

American Strategic Decline Analogy." *International Affairs* 91, issue 2 (2015): 319–31.

14. Ferguson, Niall. *Civilization: The West and the Rest*. London: Allen Lane, 2010.

15. Finney, Patrick. "Introduction: What is International History?" in *Palgrave Advances in International History*, edited by Patrick Finney. Basingstoke: Palgrave Macmillan, 2005: 1–36.

16. Fukuyama, Francis. *The End of History and the Last Man*. New York: Free Press, 2006.

17. Gaddis, John Lewis. "The Long Peace: Elements of Stability in the Postwar International System." *International Security* 10, no. 4 (1986): 99–142.

18. ____. "International Relations Theory and the End of the Cold War."*International Security* 17, no. 3 (1992): 5–58.

19. Garthoff, Raymond L. *The Great Transition: American–Soviet Relations and the End of the Cold War*. Washington, DC: Brookings Institution, 1994.

20. Herodotus, *Histories*. Translated by A. M. Bowie. Cambridge: Cambridge University Press, 2007.

21. Huntington, Samuel. "The US: Decline or Renewal?" *Foreign Affairs* 67, no. 2 (1988): 76–96.

22. Ikenberry, John. "Imperial Overstretch?" *The Economist*, June 27, 2002. Accessed September 12, 2015. http://www.economist.com/node/1188741.

23. ____. "Review of *Parliament of Man*." *Foreign Affairs* 85, no. 6 (2006): 156.

24. Kennedy, Paul. *The Rise and Fall of British Naval Mastery*. London: Allen Lane, 1976.

25. ____. *The Rise of the Anglo-German Antagonism: 1860–1914*. London: George Allen & Unwin, 1980.

26. ____. *The Rise and Fall of the Great Powers*. New York: Vintage Books, 1989.

27. ____. *Preparing for the 21st Century*. New York: Random House, 1993.

28. ____. "The Eagle Has Landed." *Financial Times*, February 1, 2002.

29. ____. *The Parliament of Man: The Past, Present, and Future of the United Nations*. New York: Random House, 2006.

30. ____. "The Distant Horizon: What Can 'Big History' Tell Us About America's Future?" *Foreign Affairs* 87, no. 3 (2008): 126–32.

31. ____. "The Imperial Mind: A Historian's Education in the Ways of Empire." *The Atlantic*, January 2008. Accessed September 3, 2015. http://www.theatlantic.com/magazine/archive/2008/01/the-imperial-mind/306566/.

32. ____. "American Power is on the Wane." *Wall Street Journal*, January 1, 2009. Accessed September 14, 2015. http://www.wsj.com/articles/SB123189377673479433.

33. ____. "Asia's Rise: Rise and Fall." *The World Today* 66, no. 8/9 (2010): 6–9.

34. Kennedy, Paul, and Edward Luttwak. "*The Rise and Fall of the Great Powers*: An Exchange." *American Scholar* 59, no. 2 (1990): 283–9.

35. Kennedy, Paul, Richard Perle, and Joseph Nye, Jr. "The Reluctant Empire: In a Time of Great Consequence." *Brown Journal of World Affairs* 10, no. 1 (2003): 11–31.

36. Knutsen, Tobjorn. *History of International Relations Theory*. Manchester: Manchester University Press, 1997.

37. Krauthammer, Charles. "The Unipolar Moment." *Foreign Affairs* 70, no. 1 (1990/91): 23–33.

38. Kupchan, Charles. "Empire, Military Power, and Economic Decline." *International Security* 13, no. 4 (1989): 36–53.

39. LaFeber, Walter. *America, Russia, and the Cold War, 1945–2002*. New York: McGraw Hill, 2002.

40. von Laue, Theodore H. *Leopold Ranke: The Formative Years*. Princeton, NJ: Princeton University Press, 1950.

41. Layne, Christopher. "The End of the Pax Americana: How Western Decline Became Inevitable." *The Atlantic*, April 2012. Accessed September 14, 2015. http://www.theatlantic.com/international/archive/2012/04/the-end-of-pax-

americana-how-western-decline-became-inevitable/256388/.

42. Lebow, Richard Ned, and Janice Gross Stein. "Reagan and the Russians." *Atlantic Monthly*, February 1994. Accessed September 12, 2015. http://www. theatlantic.com/past/politics/foreign/reagrus.htm.

43. Lieberthal, Kenneth, and Wang Jisi. *Addressing US–China Strategic Distrust.* Washington, DC: Brookings Institution, 2012.

44. McNeill, William. "*The Rise of the West* After Twenty-five Years, " *Journal of World History* 1, no. 1 (1990): 1–21.

45. ____. *The Rise of the West: A History of the Human Community.* Chicago: University of Chicago Press, 1991.

46. Nau, Henry. "Why *The Rise and Fall of the Great Powers* Was Wrong." *Review of International Studies* 27, no. 4 (2001): 579–92.

47. Nye, Jr., Joseph. "The Changing Nature of World Power." *Political Science Quarterly* 105, issue 2 (1990): 177–92.

48. ____. "Soft Power, " *Foreign Policy* no. 80 (1990): 153–71.

49. Posen, Barry. "Pull Back: The Case for a Less Activist Foreign Policy." *Foreign Affairs* 92, no. 1 (2013): 116–28.

50. von Ranke, Leopold. *History of the Latin and Teutonic Peoples 1494–1514.* Translated by G. R. Dennis. London: George Bell and Sons, 1909.

51. Richards, Huw. "Redrawing the Big Picture." *Times Higher Education*, August 28, 2008. Accessed September 2, 2015, https://www.timeshighereducation.co.uk/ features/redrawing-the-big-picture/403290.article.

52. Richardson, J. L. "Paul Kennedy and International Relations Theory: A Comparison with Robert Gilpin." *Australian Journal of International Affairs* 45, no. 1 (1991): 70–7.

53. Roberts, M. "The Military Revolution, 1560–1600." In *Essays in Swedish History*, edited by M. Roberts. London: Weidenfeld & Nicolson, 1967: 195–226.

54. Robinson, Ronald, John Gallagher, and Alice Denny. *Africa and the Victorians: The Official Mind of Imperialism*. Basingstoke: Macmillan, 1981.

55. Rostow, W. W. "Beware of Historians Bearing False Analogies." *Foreign Affairs* 66, no. 4 (1988): 863–8.

56. Schulin, Ernst. "Ranke's Universal History and National History." *Syracuse Scholar* 9, issue 1 (1988): 1–8.

57. Spengler, Oswald. *The Decline of the West*. Edited by Helmut Werner. Translated by Charles F. Atkinson. Oxford: Oxford University Press, 1991.

58. Taylor, A. J. P. *The Struggle for Mastery in Europe 1848–1918*. Oxford: Oxford University Press, 1969.

59. Thucydides. *History of the Peloponnesian War*. Edited and translated by Jeremy Mynott. Cambridge: Cambridge University Press, 2013.

60. Toynbee, Arnold. *A Study of History: Abridgement of Volumes I–VI*. Edited by D. C. Somerwell. Oxford: Oxford University Press, 1987.

61. Wallerstein, Immanuel. *The Modern World System I: Capitalist Agriculture and the Origins of the European World-Economy in the Sixteenth Century, with a New Prologue*. Berkeley: University of California Press, 2011.

62. Waltz, Kenneth. *Theory of International Politics*. Reading: Addison Wesley, 1979.

63. Zakaria, Fareed. *The Post-American World*. New York: W. W. Norton and Company, 2008.

原书作者简介

历史学家保罗·肯尼迪于 1945 年二战即将结束时出生于英格兰北部的一个工薪家庭。他是家里第一个上大学的人，本科就读于纽卡斯尔大学，后又进入牛津大学继续深造，最终获得博士学位。肯尼迪在成长过程中亲身经历了大英帝国的衰落。因此，探究大国衰落的原因就成了他毕生的追求。他的职业生涯主要是在美国耶鲁大学度过的，曾任耶鲁大学国际关系史研究室主任。肯尼迪还是一位备受尊敬的全球事务评论家和作家，同时他也为联合国和美国提供咨询服务。2001 年，他曾获大英帝国司令勋章。

本书作者简介

赖利·奎因获伦敦政治经济学院和牛津大学政治学与国际关系硕士学位。

世界名著中的批判性思维

《世界思想宝库钥匙丛书》致力于深入浅出地阐释全世界著名思想家的观点，不论是谁、在何处都能了解到，从而推进批判性思维发展。

《世界思想宝库钥匙丛书》与世界顶尖大学的一流学者合作，为一系列学科中最有影响的著作推出新的分析文本，介绍其观点和影响。在这一不断扩展的系列中，每种选入的著作都代表了历经时间考验的思想典范。通过为这些著作提供必要背景、揭示原作者的学术渊源以及说明这些著作所产生的影响，本系列图书希望让读者以新视角看待这些划时代的经典之作。读者应学会思考、运用并挑战这些著作中的观点，而不是简单接受它们。

ABOUT THE AUTHOR OF THE ORIGINAL WORK

Born in the north of England in 1945, towards the end of World War II, historian **Paul Kennedy** was the first person in his working-class family to attend university. He earned a degree at Newcastle University and went on to gain a Ph.D. from Oxford. Watching the British Empire shrink as he grew up, Kennedy developed a lifelong interest in the factors that cause great powers to wither. He has spent the majority of his career teaching in the United States, where he chaired the international history department at Yale. Kennedy has become a respected commentator and writer on global affairs, as well as advising both the United Nations and the United States. He was made a Commander of the Order of the British Empire in 2001.

ABOUT THE AUTHOR OF THE ANALYSIS

Riley Quinn holds master's degrees in politics and international relations from both LSE and the University of Oxford.

ABOUT MACAT
GREAT WORKS FOR CRITICAL THINKING

Macat is focused on making the ideas of the world's great thinkers accessible and comprehensible to everybody, everywhere, in ways that promote the development of enhanced critical thinking skills.

It works with leading academics from the world's top universities to produce new analyses that focus on the ideas and the impact of the most influential works ever written across a wide variety of academic disciplines. Each of the works that sit at the heart of its growing library is an enduring example of great thinking. But by setting them in context — and looking at the influences that shaped their authors, as well as the responses they provoked — Macat encourages readers to look at these classics and game-changers with fresh eyes. Readers learn to think, engage and challenge their ideas, rather than simply accepting them.

批判性思维与《大国的兴衰》

首要批判性思维技巧：解决问题
次要批判性思维技巧：评估

　　保罗·肯尼迪根据编辑的建议，在他研究自西班牙腓力二世以来造成欧洲大国兴衰变化原因的专著中，又多增加了一章。新加入的这一章内容意义非同寻常，这是作为历史学家的肯尼迪在对未来进行预测。在该章中，作者探讨了美国是否会和历史上那些曾经的帝国一样最终难逃衰落的命运。也正是因为有了该章内容，《大国的兴衰》竟然成了华盛顿政要在派对上经常聊到的话题，肯尼迪这位公共知识分子也因此跻身于国家政策顾问之列。

　　从严格的学术角度讲，肯尼迪的研究工作成效还体现在其他方面。尤其值得称道的是，他以问题解决者的身份提出了非常现实的问题。肯尼迪采用的是目前已经少有人在用的比较历史学研究方法，该方法可以摆脱国别史和断代史研究的局限，进而发现造成不同国家兴衰成败的共同原因。

　　《大国的兴衰》提出了著名的"帝国过度扩张"概念，这也是该书最大的贡献。肯尼迪认为所有帝国的衰落大抵都会经历如下过程：崛起的帝国在军事投入上最终超出了其经济承受能力，而其经济失去竞争优势后，整个帝国便会走向衰落。之前可能也有历史学家发现过这一规律，甚至将其用于对特定时期特定国家的研究之中。而肯尼迪这位问题解决者则用这一规律对近五百年全球大国的兴衰变化作了分析，其独到的见解令人信服。

CRITICAL THINKING AND *THE RISE AND FALL OF THE GREAT POWERS*

- Primary critical thinking skill: PROBLEM-SOLVING
- Secondary critical thinking skill: EVALUATION

Paul Kennedy owes a great deal to the editor who persuaded him to add a final chapter to this study of the factors that contributed to the rise and fall of European powers since the age of Spain's Philip II. This tailpiece indulged in what was, for an historian, a most unusual activity: it looked into the future. Pondering whether the United States would ultimately suffer the same decline as every imperium that preceded it, it was this chapter that made *The Rise and Fall of the Great Powers* a dinner party talking point in Washington government circles. In so doing, it elevated Kennedy to the ranks of public intellectuals whose opinions were canvassed on matters of state policy.

From a strictly academic point of view, the virtues of Kennedy's work lie elsewhere, and specifically in his flair for asking the sort of productive questions that characterize a great problem-solver. Kennedy's work is an example of an increasingly rare genre—a work of comparative history that transcends the narrow confines of state- and era-specific studies to identify the common factors that underpin the successes and failures of highly disparate states.

Kennedy's prime contribution is the now-famous concept of 'imperial overstretch,' the idea that empires fall largely because the military commitments they acquire during the period of their rise ultimately become too much to sustain once they lose the economic competitive edge that had projected them to dominance in the first place. Earlier historians may have glimpsed this central truth, and even applied it in studies of specific polities, but it took a problem-solver of Kennedy's ability to extend the analysis convincingly across half a millennium.

《世界思想宝库钥匙丛书》简介

《世界思想宝库钥匙丛书》致力于为一系列在各领域产生重大影响的人文社科类经典著作提供独特的学术探讨。每一本读物都不仅仅是原经典著作的内容摘要，而是介绍并深入研究原经典著作的学术渊源、主要观点和历史影响。这一丛书的目的是提供一套学习资料，以促进读者掌握批判性思维，从而更全面、深刻地去理解重要思想。

每一本读物分为 3 个部分：学术渊源、学术思想和学术影响，每个部分下有 4 个小节。这些章节旨在从各个方面研究原经典著作及其反响。

由于独特的体例，每一本读物不但易于阅读，而且另有一项优点：所有读物的编排体例相同，读者在进行某个知识层面的调查或研究时可交叉参阅多本该丛书中的相关读物，从而开启跨领域研究的路径。

为了方便阅读，每本读物最后还列出了术语表和人名表（在书中则以星号 * 标记），此外还有参考文献。

《世界思想宝库钥匙丛书》与剑桥大学合作，理清了批判性思维的要点，即如何通过 6 种技能来进行有效思考。其中 3 种技能让我们能够理解问题，另 3 种技能让我们有能力解决问题。这 6 种技能合称为"批判性思维 PACIER 模式"，它们是：

分析：了解如何建立一个观点；
评估：研究一个观点的优点和缺点；
阐释：对意义所产生的问题加以理解；
创造性思维：提出新的见解，发现新的联系；
解决问题：提出切实有效的解决办法；
理性化思维：创建有说服力的观点。

THE MACAT LIBRARY

The Macat Library is a series of unique academic explorations of seminal works in the humanities and social sciences — books and papers that have had a significant and widely recognised impact on their disciplines. It has been created to serve as much more than just a summary of what lies between the covers of a great book. It illuminates and explores the influences on, ideas of, and impact of that book. Our goal is to offer a learning resource that encourages critical thinking and fosters a better, deeper understanding of important ideas.

Each publication is divided into three Sections: Influences, Ideas, and Impact. Each Section has four Modules. These explore every important facet of the work, and the responses to it.

This Section-Module structure makes a Macat Library book easy to use, but it has another important feature. Because each Macat book is written to the same format, it is possible (and encouraged!) to cross-reference multiple Macat books along the same lines of inquiry or research. This allows the reader to open up interesting interdisciplinary pathways.

To further aid your reading, lists of glossary terms and people mentioned are included at the end of this book (these are indicated by an asterisk [*] throughout) — as well as a list of works cited.

Macat has worked with the University of Cambridge to identify the elements of critical thinking and understand the ways in which six different skills combine to enable effective thinking.

Three allow us to fully understand a problem; three more give us the tools to solve it. Together, these six skills make up the PACIER model of critical thinking. They are:

ANALYSIS — understanding how an argument is built
EVALUATION — exploring the strengths and weaknesses of an argument
INTERPRETATION — understanding issues of meaning
CREATIVE THINKING — coming up with new ideas and fresh connections
PROBLEM-SOLVING — producing strong solutions
REASONING — creating strong arguments

"《世界思想宝库钥匙丛书》提供了独一无二的跨学科学习和研究工具。它介绍那些革新了各自学科研究的经典著作，还邀请全世界一流专家和教育机构进行严谨的分析，为每位读者打开世界顶级教育的大门。"

——安德烈亚斯·施莱歇尔，
经济合作与发展组织教育与技能司司长

"《世界思想宝库钥匙丛书》直面大学教育的巨大挑战……他们组建了一支精干而活跃的学者队伍，来推出在研究广度上颇具新意的教学材料。"

——布罗尔斯教授、勋爵，剑桥大学前校长

"《世界思想宝库钥匙丛书》的愿景令人赞叹。它通过分析和阐释那些曾深刻影响人类思想以及社会、经济发展的经典文本，提供了新的学习方法。它推动批判性思维，这对于任何社会和经济体来说都是至关重要的。这就是未来的学习方法。"

——查尔斯·克拉克阁下，英国前教育大臣

"对于那些影响了各自领域的著作，《世界思想宝库钥匙丛书》能让人们立即了解到围绕那些著作展开的评论性言论，这让该系列图书成为在这些领域从事研究的师生们不可或缺的资源。"

——威廉·特朗佐教授，加利福尼亚大学圣地亚哥分校

"Macat offers an amazing first-of-its-kind tool for interdisciplinary learning and research. Its focus on works that transformed their disciplines and its rigorous approach, drawing on the world's leading experts and educational institutions, opens up a world-class education to anyone."

—— Andreas Schleicher, Director for Education and Skills, Organisation for Economic Co-operation and Development

"Macat is taking on some of the major challenges in university education... They have drawn together a strong team of active academics who are producing teaching materials that are novel in the breadth of their approach."

—— Prof Lord Broers, former Vice-Chancellor of the University of Cambridge

"The Macat vision is exceptionally exciting. It focuses upon new modes of learning which analyse and explain seminal texts which have profoundly influenced world thinking and so social and economic development. It promotes the kind of critical thinking which is essential for any society and economy. This is the learning of the future."

—— Rt Hon Charles Clarke, former UK Secretary of State for Education

"The Macat analyses provide immediate access to the critical conversation surrounding the books that have shaped their respective discipline, which will make them an invaluable resource to all of those, students and teachers, working in the field."

—— Prof William Tronzo, University of California at San Diego

The Macat Library
世界思想宝库钥匙丛书

TITLE	中文书名	类别
An Analysis of Arjun Appadurai's *Modernity at Large: Cultural Dimensions of Globalization*	解析阿尔君·阿帕杜莱《消失的现代性：全球化的文化维度》	人类学
An Analysis of Claude Lévi-Strauss's *Structural Anthropology*	解析克劳德·列维-斯特劳斯《结构人类学》	人类学
An Analysis of Marcel Mauss's *The Gift*	解析马塞尔·莫斯《礼物》	人类学
An Analysis of Jared M. Diamond's *Guns, Germs, and Steel: The Fate of Human Societies*	解析贾雷德·M.戴蒙德《枪炮、病菌与钢铁：人类社会的命运》	人类学
An Analysis of Clifford Geertz's *The Interpretation of Cultures*	解析克利福德·格尔茨《文化的解释》	人类学
An Analysis of Philippe Ariès's *Centuries of Childhood: A Social History of Family Life*	解析菲力浦·阿利埃斯《儿童的世纪：旧制度下的儿童和家庭生活》	人类学
An Analysis of W. Chan Kim & Renée Mauborgne's *Blue Ocean Strategy*	解析金伟灿/勒妮·莫博涅《蓝海战略》	商业
An Analysis of John P. Kotter's *Leading Change*	解析约翰·P.科特《领导变革》	商业
An Analysis of Michael E. Porter's *Competitive Strategy: Techniques for Analyzing Industries and Competitors*	解析迈克尔·E.波特《竞争战略：分析产业和竞争对手的技术》	商业
An Analysis of Jean Lave & Etienne Wenger's *Situated Learning: Legitimate Peripheral Participation*	解析琼·莱夫/艾蒂纳·温格《情境学习：合法的边缘性参与》	商业
An Analysis of Douglas McGregor's *The Human Side of Enterprise*	解析道格拉斯·麦格雷戈《企业的人性面》	商业
An Analysis of Milton Friedman's *Capitalism and Freedom*	解析米尔顿·弗里德曼《资本主义与自由》	商业
An Analysis of Ludwig von Mises's *The Theory of Money and Credit*	解析路德维希·冯·米塞斯《货币和信用理论》	经济学
An Analysis of Adam Smith's *The Wealth of Nations*	解析亚当·斯密《国富论》	经济学
An Analysis of Thomas Piketty's *Capital in the Twenty-First Century*	解析托马斯·皮凯蒂《21世纪资本论》	经济学
An Analysis of Nassim Nicholas Taleb's *The Black Swan: The Impact of the Highly Improbable*	解析纳西姆·尼古拉斯·塔勒布《黑天鹅：如何应对不可预知的未来》	经济学
An Analysis of Ha-Joon Chang's *Kicking Away the Ladder*	解析张夏准《富国陷阱：发达国家为何踢开梯子》	经济学
An Analysis of Thomas Robert Malthus's *An Essay on the Principle of Population*	解析托马斯·罗伯特·马尔萨斯《人口论》	经济学

An Analysis of John Maynard Keynes's *The General Theory of Employment, Interest and Money*	解析约翰·梅纳德·凯恩斯《就业、利息和货币通论》	经济学
An Analysis of Milton Friedman's *The Role of Monetary Policy*	解析米尔顿·弗里德曼《货币政策的作用》	经济学
An Analysis of Burton G. Malkiel's *A Random Walk Down Wall Street*	解析伯顿·G.马尔基尔《漫步华尔街》	经济学
An Analysis of Friedrich A. Hayek's *The Road to Serfdom*	解析弗里德里希·A.哈耶克《通往奴役之路》	经济学
An Analysis of Charles P. Kindleberger's *Manias, Panics, and Crashes: A History of Financial Crises*	解析查尔斯·P.金德尔伯格《疯狂、惊恐和崩溃：金融危机史》	经济学
An Analysis of Amartya Sen's *Development as Freedom*	解析阿马蒂亚·森《以自由看待发展》	经济学
An Analysis of Rachel Carson's *Silent Spring*	解析蕾切尔·卡森《寂静的春天》	地理学
An Analysis of Charles Darwin's *On the Origin of Species: by Means of Natural Selection, or The Preservation of Favoured Races in the Struggle for Life*	解析查尔斯·达尔文《物种起源》	地理学
An Analysis of World Commission on Environment and Development's *The Brundtland Report, Our Common Future*	解析世界环境与发展委员会《布伦特兰报告：我们共同的未来》	地理学
An Analysis of James E. Lovelock's *Gaia: A New Look at Life on Earth*	解析詹姆斯·E.拉伍洛克《盖娅：地球生命的新视野》	地理学
An Analysis of Paul Kennedy's *The Rise and Fall of the Great Powers: Economic Change and Military Conflict from 1500–2000*	解析保罗·肯尼迪《大国的兴衰：1500—2000年的经济变革与军事冲突》	历史
An Analysis of Janet L. Abu-Lughod's *Before European Hegemony: The World System A. D. 1250–1350*	解析珍妮特·L.阿布-卢格霍德《欧洲霸权之前：1250—1350年的世界体系》	历史
An Analysis of Alfred W. Crosby's *The Columbian Exchange: Biological and Cultural Consequences of 1492*	解析艾尔弗雷德·W.克罗斯比《哥伦布大交换：1492年以后的生物影响和文化冲击》	历史
An Analysis of Tony Judt's *Postwar: A History of Europe since 1945*	解析托尼·朱特《战后欧洲史》	历史
An Analysis of Richard J. Evans's *In Defence of History*	解析理查德·J.艾文斯《捍卫历史》	历史
An Analysis of Eric Hobsbawm's *The Age of Revolution: Europe 1789–1848*	解析艾瑞克·霍布斯鲍姆《革命的年代：欧洲1789—1848年》	历史

An Analysis of Roland Barthes's *Mythologies*	解析罗兰·巴特《神话学》	文学与批判理论
An Analysis of Simone de Beauvoir's *The Second Sex*	解析西蒙娜·德·波伏娃《第二性》	文学与批判理论
An Analysis of Edward W. Said's *Orientalism*	解析爱德华·W. 萨义德《东方主义》	文学与批判理论
An Analysis of Virginia Woolf's *A Room of One's Own*	解析弗吉尼亚·伍尔芙《一间自己的房间》	文学与批判理论
An Analysis of Judith Butler's *Gender Trouble*	解析朱迪斯·巴特勒《性别麻烦》	文学与批判理论
An Analysis of Ferdinand de Saussure's *Course in General Linguistics*	解析费尔迪南·德·索绪尔《普通语言学教程》	文学与批判理论
An Analysis of Susan Sontag's *On Photography*	解析苏珊·桑塔格《论摄影》	文学与批判理论
An Analysis of Walter Benjamin's *The Work of Art in the Age of Mechanical Reproduction*	解析瓦尔特·本雅明《机械复制时代的艺术作品》	文学与批判理论
An Analysis of W. E. B. Du Bois's *The Souls of Black Folk*	解析 W.E.B. 杜波依斯《黑人的灵魂》	文学与批判理论
An Analysis of Plato's *The Republic*	解析柏拉图《理想国》	哲学
An Analysis of Plato's *Symposium*	解析柏拉图《会饮篇》	哲学
An Analysis of Aristotle's *Metaphysics*	解析亚里士多德《形而上学》	哲学
An Analysis of Aristotle's *Nicomachean Ethics*	解析亚里士多德《尼各马可伦理学》	哲学
An Analysis of Immanuel Kant's *Critique of Pure Reason*	解析伊曼努尔·康德《纯粹理性批判》	哲学
An Analysis of Ludwig Wittgenstein's *Philosophical Investigations*	解析路德维希·维特根斯坦《哲学研究》	哲学
An Analysis of G. W. F. Hegel's *Phenomenology of Spirit*	解析 G.W.F. 黑格尔《精神现象学》	哲学
An Analysis of Baruch Spinoza's *Ethics*	解析巴鲁赫·斯宾诺莎《伦理学》	哲学
An Analysis of Hannah Arendt's *The Human Condition*	解析汉娜·阿伦特《人的境况》	哲学
An Analysis of G. E. M. Anscombe's *Modern Moral Philosophy*	解析 G.E.M. 安斯康姆《现代道德哲学》	哲学
An Analysis of David Hume's *An Enquiry Concerning Human Understanding*	解析大卫·休谟《人类理解研究》	哲学

An Analysis of Søren Kierkegaard's *Fear and Trembling*	解析索伦·克尔凯郭尔《恐惧与战栗》	哲学
An Analysis of René Descartes's *Meditations on First Philosophy*	解析勒内·笛卡尔《第一哲学沉思录》	哲学
An Analysis of Friedrich Nietzsche's *On the Genealogy of Morality*	解析弗里德里希·尼采《论道德的谱系》	哲学
An Analysis of Gilbert Ryle's *The Concept of Mind*	解析吉尔伯特·赖尔《心的概念》	哲学
An Analysis of Thomas Kuhn's *The Structure of Scientific Revolutions*	解析托马斯·库恩《科学革命的结构》	哲学
An Analysis of John Stuart Mill's *Utilitarianism*	解析约翰·斯图亚特·穆勒《功利主义》	哲学
An Analysis of Aristotle's *Politics*	解析亚里士多德《政治学》	政治学
An Analysis of Niccolò Machiavelli's *The Prince*	解析尼科洛·马基雅维利《君主论》	政治学
An Analysis of Karl Marx's *Capital*	解析卡尔·马克思《资本论》	政治学
An Analysis of Benedict Anderson's *Imagined Communities*	解析本尼迪克特·安德森《想象的共同体》	政治学
An Analysis of Samuel P. Huntington's *The Clash of Civilizations and the Remaking of World Order*	解析塞缪尔·P.亨廷顿《文明的冲突与世界秩序的重建》	政治学
An Analysis of Alexis de Tocqueville's *Democracy in America*	解析阿列克西·德·托克维尔《论美国的民主》	政治学
An Analysis of John A. Hobson's *Imperialism: A Study*	解析约翰·A.霍布森《帝国主义》	政治学
An Analysis of Thomas Paine's *Common Sense*	解析托马斯·潘恩《常识》	政治学
An Analysis of John Rawls's *A Theory of Justice*	解析约翰·罗尔斯《正义论》	政治学
An Analysis of Francis Fukuyama's *The End of History and the Last Man*	解析弗朗西斯·福山《历史的终结与最后的人》	政治学
An Analysis of John Locke's *Two Treatises of Government*	解析约翰·洛克《政府论》	政治学
An Analysis of Sun Tzu's *The Art of War*	解析孙武《孙子兵法》	政治学
An Analysis of Henry Kissinger's *World Order: Reflections on the Character of Nations and the Course of History*	解析亨利·基辛格《世界秩序》	政治学
An Analysis of Jean-Jacques Rousseau's *The Social Contract*	解析让-雅克·卢梭《社会契约论》	政治学

An Analysis of Odd Arne Westad's *The Global Cold War: Third World Interventions and the Making of Our Times*	解析文安立《全球冷战：美苏对第三世界的干涉与当代世界的形成》	政治学
An Analysis of Sigmund Freud's *The Interpretation of Dreams*	解析西格蒙德·弗洛伊德《梦的解析》	心理学
An Analysis of William James' *The Principles of Psychology*	解析威廉·詹姆斯《心理学原理》	心理学
An Analysis of Philip Zimbardo's *The Lucifer Effect*	解析菲利普·津巴多《路西法效应》	心理学
An Analysis of Leon Festinger's *A Theory of Cognitive Dissonance*	解析利昂·费斯汀格《认知失调论》	心理学
An Analysis of Richard H. Thaler & Cass R. Sunstein's *Nudge: Improving Decisions about Health, Wealth, and Happiness*	解析理查德·H.泰勒/卡斯·R.桑斯坦《助推：如何做出有关健康、财富和幸福的更优决策》	心理学
An Analysis of Gordon Allport's *The Nature of Prejudice*	解析高尔登·奥尔波特《偏见的本质》	心理学
An Analysis of Steven Pinker's *The Better Angels of Our Nature: Why Violence Has Declined*	解析斯蒂芬·平克《人性中的善良天使：暴力为什么会减少》	心理学
An Analysis of Stanley Milgram's *Obedience to Authority*	解析斯坦利·米尔格拉姆《对权威的服从》	心理学
An Analysis of Betty Friedan's *The Feminine Mystique*	解析贝蒂·弗里丹《女性的奥秘》	心理学
An Analysis of David Riesman's *The Lonely Crowd: A Study of the Changing American Character*	解析大卫·理斯曼《孤独的人群：美国人社会性格演变之研究》	社会学
An Analysis of Franz Boas's *Race, Language and Culture*	解析弗朗兹·博厄斯《种族、语言与文化》	社会学
An Analysis of Pierre Bourdieu's *Outline of a Theory of Practice*	解析皮埃尔·布尔厄《实践理论大纲》	社会学
An Analysis of Max Weber's *The Protestant Ethic and the Spirit of Capitalism*	解析马克斯·韦伯《新教伦理与资本主义精神》	社会学
An Analysis of Jane Jacobs's *The Death and Life of Great American Cities*	解析简·雅各布斯《美国大城市的死与生》	社会学
An Analysis of C. Wright Mills's *The Sociological Imagination*	解析C.赖特·米尔斯《社会学的想象力》	社会学
An Analysis of Robert E. Lucas Jr.'s *Why Doesn't Capital Flow from Rich to Poor Countries?*	解析小罗伯特·E.卢卡斯《为何资本不从富国流向穷国？》	社会学

An Analysis of Émile Durkheim's *On Suicide*	解析埃米尔·迪尔凯姆《自杀论》	社会学
An Analysis of Eric Hoffer's *The True Believer: Thoughts on the Nature of Mass Movements*	解析埃里克·霍弗《狂热分子：群众运动圣经》	社会学
An Analysis of Jared M. Diamond's *Collapse: How Societies Choose to Fail or Survive*	解析贾雷德·M.戴蒙德《大崩溃：社会如何选择兴亡》	社会学
An Analysis of Michel Foucault's *The History of Sexuality Vol. 1: The Will to Knowledge*	解析米歇尔·福柯《性史（第一卷）：求知意志》	社会学
An Analysis of Michel Foucault's *Discipline and Punish*	解析米歇尔·福柯《规训与惩罚》	社会学
An Analysis of Richard Dawkins's *The Selfish Gene*	解析理查德·道金斯《自私的基因》	社会学
An Analysis of Antonio Gramsci's *Prison Notebooks*	解析安东尼奥·葛兰西《狱中札记》	社会学
An Analysis of Augustine's *Confessions*	解析奥古斯丁《忏悔录》	神学
An Analysis of C. S. Lewis's *The Abolition of Man*	解析 C. S. 路易斯《人之废》	神学

图书在版编目（CIP）数据

解析保罗·肯尼迪《大国的兴衰：1500—2000年的经济变革与军事冲突》：汉、英 / 赖利·奎恩(Riley Quinn) 著；王晋瑞译. —上海：上海外语教育出版社，2020
（世界思想宝库钥匙丛书）
ISBN 978-7-5446-6140-9

Ⅰ.①解… Ⅱ.①赖… ②王… Ⅲ.①国际政治－研究－1500—2000－汉、英 ②世界经济－研究－1500—2000－汉、英 ③国际关系史－研究－1500—2000－汉、英 Ⅳ.①D5 ②F11 ③D819

中国版本图书馆CIP数据核字（2020）第022640号

This Chinese-English bilingual edition of *An Analysis of Paul Kennedy's* The Rise and Fall of the Great Powers: Economic Change and Military Conflict from 1500—2000 is published by arrangement with Macat International Limited.
Licensed for sale throughout the world.

本书汉英双语版由Macat国际有限公司授权上海外语教育出版社有限公司出版。供在全世界范围内发行、销售。

图字：09 – 2018 – 549

出版发行：**上海外语教育出版社**
（上海外国语大学内） 邮编：200083
电　　话：021-65425300（总机）
电子邮箱：bookinfo@sflep.com.cn
网　　址：http://www.sflep.com
责任编辑：王　璐

印　　刷：上海叶大印务发展有限公司
开　　本：890×1240　1/32　印张 6.25　字数 128千字
版　　次：2020 年 7 月第 1 版　2020 年 7 月第 1 次印刷
印　　数：2 100 册

书　　号：ISBN 978-7-5446-6140-9
定　　价：30.00 元

本版图书如有印装质量问题，可向本社调换
质量服务热线：4008-213-263　电子邮箱：editorial@sflep.com